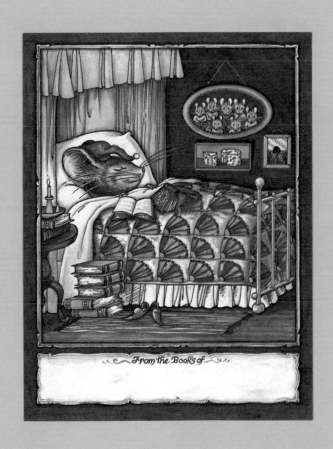

From the Books of

NEW DESIGNS FOR MACHINE PATCHWORK

NEW DESIGNS FOR MACHINE PATCHWORK

MURIEL HIGGINS

Charles Scribner's Sons
New York

Acknowledgments

First of all I have to acknowledge the interest shown in my patchwork by a huge range of friends and acquaintances in Britain and overseas.

Specifically I should thank Deirdre Amsden of Cambridge, whose work confirms the validity of machine patchwork and inspired me to my first serious quilting. William McClelland and Patricia King helped me to sort out some of the bidialectal difficulties of catering for both British and American readers, and made several helpful suggestions. Ann Greaves drew a lot of the diagrams, coping constructively with sketchy directions and misplaced lines. My editor Pauline Stride has been from the beginning a cheerful and helpful adviser.

My husband John took the photographs and has always been ready with a sympathetic ear when I have needed one. Our daughters Anna and Jenny have borne with me in many a museum while I've scribbled down designs and patterns. And finally, if Anna hadn't got mumps on our first morning in Egypt in July 1977, with Jenny following three weeks later, we would never together have made a hand patchwork of over 2000 hexagons in random colours; and this, perhaps more than anything else, convinced me by its design shortcomings of the virtues of planning.

Alexandria   Muriel Higgins
July 1979

CONTENTS

INTRODUCTION

The general term patchwork covers two kinds of work : appliqué or applied work, where pieces of material are applied or put on to a ground fabric; and mosaic patchwork, where an area of fabric is constructed by joining together a number of pieces of material (which may be of different shapes and sizes). More correctly called piecework, mosaic patchwork is also sometimes referred to as geometric patchwork. This book is about designs for mosaic patchwork.

Traditionally mosaic patchwork as practised in Britain and North America has been done by hand, although sewing machines are said to have been used in America from the time they became common items of domestic equipment. Hand patchwork — of which many fine examples, both old and modern, can be found on both sides of the Atlantic — bespeaks industry and persistence, as well as ingenuity and skill in piecing and sewing and in many cases a well-developed sense of design. But for every completed hand patchwork, there must be several given up in despair at the prospect of the work involved, from lack of continuing interest, or because of failure or shortcomings in planning and design. I make no apologies for offering here planned designs for patchwork by machine; being in general faster, machine work gives you a better chance of completing a project. Although the designs are presented for machine sewing, they can of course also be sewn by hand if you prefer.

The designs are at once old and new. They are old in that many of them are based on Islamic decoration, where they can be found in many different media, including stone, plaster or stucco, brick, paint, wood, metal and ceramics. I have also included a few traditional patchwork designs : some blocks adapted for machine sewing, and some where manipulations of colouring and/or rotation in fact produce patterns observed in Islamic decoration. Certain design elements are common to all designers, and it has been one of my great joys to find the same basic designs underlying patterns with widely differing geographical origins.

The reader may wonder how these can be called new designs at all. It is for mosaic patchwork that they are new. Some of the designs and patterns may never have been sewn before, and almost certainly not in patchwork. Being capable of infinite repetition, many of them are very suitable for textile design, and have appeared throughout history in woven or printed form. Anyone interested in applied work should note that fine examples of traditional arabesque designs are made in Cairo, in the Bab Zuweila district.

As well as the designs themselves, I have also included general information on cutting and sewing for machine patchwork, and instructions about particular blocks and their assembly. However there are related subjects with which I have not dealt at length, eg quilting, which is well covered in some of the books listed. Similarly, while a few uses for patchwork are suggested, there are for instance no specific instructions for making up articles of clothing in patchwork. Again, this information is available elsewhere.

The designs, and the patterns which can be derived from them, are intended purely as a starting point. You can change them, adapt them, simplify them or elaborate them as you will. What you do with them is your personal choice. Patchwork has always been an individual skill and a very personal art, and it is right for it to remain so.

DEFINITIONS

The following terms are used throughout the book.

Block
Usually a square of pieced materials with a particular design. Some blocks are not pieced, but plain, ie consisting of one piece of material. Some blocks are rectangular or diamond-shaped.

Unit
Regular measurement along the sides of a block. A block with three units in each direction is a 3 x 3 block.

Design
Arrangement of shapes and colours within a block. This term is also used in the general abstract sense.

Pattern
Arrangement of blocks, tesselation (a term more often associated with tiles or mosaic). Many dictionaries define *design* and *pattern* in terms of each other, and I have made the arbitrary decision to use *design* within the block, and keep *pattern* for the ordered repetition of blocks.

Piece
Element of the block, material of a particular shape and size. This term is also used in its everyday sense : a piece of paper etc. The verb *to piece* means simply to sew together, to join.

Template
Shape or pattern for cutting a particular size or shape.

MEASUREMENTS

Measurements are given in centimetres (cm) and inches (in). Note that in accordance with common practice (as with weights in recipes) equivalents are approximate and not exact, so that round figures can be used in both systems. These approximations are used :

2.5cm = 1 in
5cm   = 2 in
10cm = 4 in etc.

This means, again as in recipes, that you cannot switch around between metric and imperial systems within a project : if you start with inches, you must stay with imperial measurements throughout. In a few illustrative examples, only one set of measurements is given. These are cases where the arithmetic is the important feature, and clarity would not be increased by quoting two sets of figures.

DIFFERENCES BETWEEN HAND AND MACHINE PATCHWORK

HAND PATCHWORK

If you want to do patchwork by hand in the traditional English way, you start with firm paper or light card. (I have called this the 'traditional' way although papers have not always been used.) From the paper or card you cut out a supply of 'papers' cut accurately to your pattern, the exact size of the finished patch. Then, from material, you cut pieces which are bigger than the paper by the amount of the seam allowance on all sides. A material piece is laid over a paper shape, and pinned in place so that the seam allowance can be folded over the paper and tacked down. When several pieces have been tacked, they are joined together by oversewing from the back.

Note that it is the size of the papers that matters — the material could be any shape provided it covers the paper. However, this would be wasteful of material, and unattractive at the back, so shapes, or templates, are also used to mark the material for cutting in hand patchwork.

Americans know this method of using papers as 'English piecing'. They themselves traditionally mark seam lines on the material and judge seam allowances, joining on the seam line with a running stitch.

Joining by hand by either of these methods allows carful matching of corners by easing, and the setting-in, with care, of squares to the inside angles of L-shapes.

MACHINE PATCHWORK

Machine patchwork is close to the American method of patchwork without papers. In general terms, the pieces are cut with an exactly measured seam allowance, and then joined from the back with a straight machine seam along the sewing line. It is clear that to ensure accuracy templates are needed here too. For machine patchwork you need one template — which is used again and again — for each shape that occurs in a block. The size of the template is the size of the finished piece plus on all sides the exact seam allowance which has been decided on, a measurement that must remain constant throughout a piece of work. Whereas in hand patchwork with papers or marked seam lines there is a certain tolerance about the size of the material pieces, in machine patchwork there is no latitude in this respect, and the template used for cutting must be exact.

It should be said here that machine patchwork is not tolerant or error at any stage : cutting, sewing or assembly. Inaccurately-cut pieces of material will lead to almost insurmountable problems, and you will find that such problems usually manifest themselves in more than one way : if you adjust to take up inaccuracies when joining horizontal strips, you may have created a new set of problems when you come to join these vertically. It is always easier to throw out a badly off-square block and make a new one than to insist on using it, and similarly, easier to discard a badly-cut piece than to try to make it fit. Such problems are of course best avoided, and this can be done by careful attentiveness at all stages.

It is said that the real speed of a typist depends on how long is spent correcting errors, and the same applies to machine patchwork. Machine seams are much faster than hand seams, but a rapidly-sewn seam only saves time if it is right. The prudent maxim *Get it right the first time* should be in your thoughts.

These line are not intended to put people off machine patchwork. It is not difficult for either novice or experienced machine-user, provided care is taken at all stages. Some of the problems which may arise even with close attention can be solved, and these are dealt with later. The ill fame frequently accorded to machine patchwork — often by accomplished hand-patchworkers — probably relates to work hastily cut and assembled by people who did not realise until too late that it demands every bit as much care and attention as hand patchwork.

Constraints of machine patchwork

There are certain constraints about the types of designs which can conveniently be sewn by machine. Joining curved seams, while possible, is not easy. A machine does not happily join hexagons, with their three-way 120° joins. Setting-in to an L-shape is a problem, but one which can easily be solved by adding an extra join, that is, by piecing.

1   Piecing an L-shape

For comfortable and rewarding machine patchwork, designs must be arranged to allow straight seaming, the joining of one straight side to another. In practical terms, this means that certain types of designs are excluded entirely : anything with true curves, although some patterns may give a curved effect; and allover hexagon patterns, though hexagons occur in several patterns.

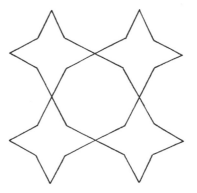

2 a   Curved effect

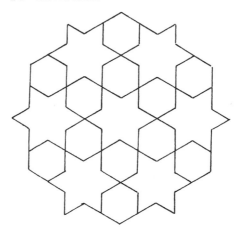

b   Pattern including hexagons

Some sources imply that machine patchwork can only be successful when squares and rectangles are used. A glance through the range of designs and patterns here and in some of the books listed in the bibliography should convince even the sceptical that this is simply not true.

Summary of procedure

The procedure for machine patchwork is as follows : for each shape in a block a template is made to include seam allowances; material is cut to the exact size of the template, and pieces are joined from the back with a straight machine stitch, building up into blocks which are finally assembled.

Note that in Britain mosaic patchwork has tended to favour the allover repetition of a single geometrical shape, sometimes with the addition of related shapes. In North America such 'one-patch' patterns have been less popular, and there the method of piecing blocks and joining them remains the more common approach. With one exception, the designs here are block designs.

MATERIALS AND EQUIPMENT

FABRIC

Let us start by thinking about fabric. Material for patchwork must be fabric which can be cut to an exact size : firmly-woven material which does not fray or stretch. You are going to join pieces together, and sometimes seams will cross, with a build-up of several layers underneath, so the material must not be too heavy in weight. Shapes should fit cleanly together, with clearly-defined joins, so you need material which will take a crease when the seams are pressed. This means that many materials with a high artificial content must be excluded, as they resist pressing and tend to be springy.

At least for early attempts at patchwork, therefore, look for material which is firmly-woven and crisp without being springy. It should be of light or light-medium weight, and preferably of natural fibres. Remember that all the materials used in a piece of work should be of the same or very similar weight and texture.

Looking through your scraps

Look through your scraps and discard all but cotton and mixtures of cotton and man-made materials (you may already know from dressmaking which of these handle well). Now consider the weight. Discard heavy materials like denim and sailcloth, and any flimsy material. You should now be left with a fairly homogeneous collection as far as weight and texture go. It is likely that you have a mixture of self-coloured materials and different types of prints of varying scale : spots, stripes, flowers, abstract and geometrical patterns etc. You must now look carefully at these printed materials.

Prints

Small-scale prints are probably best for patchwork — larger prints often work badly in combination. Before you start putting prints together, try to get an idea of how each will look cut up into small pieces, often very different from its appearance in a length. Make a viewing window of paper or cardboard so that you can isolate an area of the approximate shape or size you want to use. The pattern should still be coherent; if it is not, shift the window around to find an area which is pleasing in isolation.

One advantage of small-scale prints is that when pieces of the same material are joined, block seams are almost invisible. From this point of view, regard stripes in particular with caution. They need a lot of careful matching, and if this is not exact it can be disturbingly obvious. On the other hand, it is possible to make very effective use of stripes, using their direction to lead the eye in reading dynamic patterns.

Buying material

The weight of tradition can made people who go out and buy material for patchwork feel guilty. It would be economical and satisfying always to use only the scraps to hand, but there is little virtue in being so intent on using scraps that you finish up with an ill-assorted hodge-podge.

Often a collection of patterned scraps will benefit from the inclusion of some self-coloured material. This has a tranquillising effect on mixed scraps, which can be busy and restless in conjunction. Here you may well have to buy material of an appropriate tone.

Another case for buying material is when you want a unifying effect. The most successful random or scrap patchworks are often those which include quite a lot of a single material, plain or printed. This can act as a background, separating the different prints or colours and pulling the whole pattern together. Such material will probably have to be bought specially; watch remnant counters for suitable lengths.

Planning is one of the most important steps — though often too little respected — in a piece of patchwork. Many early patchworks were put together hastily from whatever was to hand. For reasons of availability, cost and sometimes even politics, the planned choice of materials was often an impossibility. In a more leisured and affluent age, we do not suffer from such constraints. We have time to plan in advance, and we can enjoy the luxury of choice. The purchase of material is an aspect of the overall planning which enhances the end product.

Colour and design

Light and dark tones

The design blocks are mostly drawn out in two tones, light and dark, with a third contrasting tone in some blocks. If you want to work from scraps, sort them out into darks and lights, leaving aside those you cannot decide about. You can judge tone values by looking at materials together in dim natural or artificial light or with half-closed eyes. Remember that different types of artificial lighting may affect the tone and colour relationships.

Having sorted your scraps, you can decide to use all of one group, buying the other tone so that it is unified. Motifs will then appear as varying darks on a light ground or vice versa. If you try to use both random darks and lights, then ambiguous tones will prevent or hinder the correct reading of the pattern. It is always difficult to know in advance whether patterned materials will read as dark or light in the context of other tones. Never plan to use a tone as dark in one place and light in another : a blue floral print may appear dark beside cream or beige, and light beside brown or purple, but it must be considered in its collective relationship to all the other dark and light tones.

The ability to predict how tones will work in concert is probably best learnt by trial and error. Lay out sewn blocks together, and your eye should be able to inform you of errors; it is not too late to withdraw and replace blocks which seem wrong. Something that looks wrong probably is wrong.

Choice of colours

A friend looking at my worked patchwork samples commented interestingly that although geometrical patterns may of themselves be cold and unemotional, warmth and feeling are given by one's personal choice of colour.

These following points are important in planning colouring.

If you want to make a household article, consider where it will be placed, and whether it will be happy with the surrounding colours.

The colours chosen should look pleasing together. You will not put pink and yellow together if you think they clash, certainly, but unpredictable clashes can occur, colours in isolation being different from colours put together.

You may find colour choice easier if you work initially with a limited range of colours. Various tones of a single colour can be used, or adjacent colours on the spectrum : red/orange/yellow/green/blue/purple/red. Some of the books listed in the bibliography give extensive coverage to colour theory.

If you are making a random scrap patchwork, watch carefully the *loading*, both of tones and colours — the top of the piece should not be all pinks and the bottom blues unless you planned it that way. Some kind of balance of colours is preferable.

For colours which will be adjacent in the patchwork, do not choose tones so close to each other that the effect of the pattern is lost because the eye cannot distinguish them. To check this, stand well back and see how the colours interact. Standing back and viewing from afar is always a good strategy to check up on the total effect.

Proportions

One often hears that to avoid monotony the amounts used of each colour should not be equal. Few blocks have exactly equal amounts of two tones, but many patterns produced by putting blocks together consist of interlocked motifs, often in a counterchange of dark and light. If this seems monotonous, then a border could be added, taking up one of the tones and increasing its proportions in terms of the whole. On the other hand, many Islamic patterns have their charm precisely in their ordered regularity and infinite extensibility.

How much material ?
If you are working from true scraps of irregular shapes and sizes, it will be almost impossible to work out if you have enough material (ie how many pieces can be cut) without actually setting to and cutting as many as you can. You may have a number of irregular but similarly-shaped scraps. Find our how many pieces can be cut from one scrap, and multiply by the number of scraps of that material you have. If you are short, one way you can add to the number is by more economical cutting. Or you can cut half shapes (remembering to add a seam allowance to the edges to be joined together); you can cut on the bias of the material if you have to, but such pieces have stretchy edges and distort easily, and must therefore be sewn with care.

If you are buying material by the metre or yard, or working from large pieces, you can work out roughly how much you need. See how many times a piece of the shape and size you want can be fitted across the width of the material, keeping clear of the selvages (which may pucker) and letting each piece be cut separately. Measure the length this takes and calculate how many such widths you need. Thus if you need thirty pieces, and one width yields ten, you need three widths. Round up the final figure to the next half metre or yard. If the same material is needed for another shape in the block, work it out for the second shape in the same way, adding the two figures to get the total. Round up after adding the figures.

It is a good idea to work out how much you need for widths of both 90 cm (35-6 in) and 115 cm (45 in), as these are common widths for the weight you are likely to want.

SEWING MACHINE

The choice of materials has already been discussed more patchwork probably comes out badly because of the use of unsuitable materials than for any other reason. Also, it is up to you to decide which materials to use, and if you make mistakes, they can be rectified later or at a further try. But when we come to

the next item - your sewing machine - then you are obliged to proceed with what you have.

Luckily, the demands are simple. You need a machine that sews straight seams sweetly and happily. There is no need to have a zigzag or swing-needle machine with a variety of stitches; you do not have to be able to sew in reverse direction. And if your machine has a single invariable stitch length, it is likely to be a medium stitch length, which is quite suitable. A machine of the free-arm type may have a attachable flat extension surface (called a sewing table by some manufacturers). This will give you a large flat surface to work on. Cabinet or build-in machines already offer the flat surface.

Basically you will be using the machine to sew straight seams from the back, exactly as in dress-making. Check that the needle is straight and not bent; it should also be sharp and smooth - a snag at the needle point will cause pulled threads. The needle should be the same size as you use for dressmaking with cotton (14 or European 90). If the needle holes seem large or noticeable, try a size finer needle.

Stitch length should be medium, 4 sts/cm (10 sts/in); 2-2½ on the 1-4 scale of a Bernina machine, for example. Longer stitches will not be strong enough and may come undone; shorter stitches are difficult to unpick (some mistakes are inevitable), and a tight row of needle holes can weaken the material. Fluff accumulates, so it will be necessary to clean round the bobbin case more often than usual. Make sure that the tension is exactly right, with top and bobbin threads in even tension without looping or pulling.

For sewing cotton material, use mercerised or polyester cotton thread (sizes 40 or 50, depending on the weight of the material). Silk and man-made fabrics should be sewn with matching threads. As stitches do not show at the front of the work, thread colours need not be matched exactly to the material; for joining dark to light materials, dark thread is usually preferred.

OTHER EQUIPMENT

For cutting
Dressmaking scissors or shears are required. The blades should be long to allow a clean single cut to be made along one side of a shape, and they must be sharp throughout their length. In addition, a small pair of pointed scissors is useful for snipping threads. I find scissors easier than a seam-ripper for unpicking, as I all too often rip the material instead of the seam, but many people are proficient with a seam-ripper, and prefer that.

You also need paper scissors, and scissors which will cut cardboard. Dressmaking scissors should not, of course, be used to cut paper or card or for general household purposes. For cutting templates, a craft knife (eg Versicut or X-acto knife) gives better results than scissors.

For drawing and making templates
For drawing out patterns you need squared paper, or isometric paper, which has a grid of equilateral triangles (obtainable from art supply shops used by draughtsmen — blueprint companies in the USA — and from good stationers). (See the grids given at the end of the book).

You need a supply of soft and hard pencils, an eraser and a ruler. At the design stage you can indicate tone values by pencil shading. For colour planning use coloured pencils or felt-tipped markers, though it can be difficult to find a range of subtle colours in these.

For making templates you need squared or isometric paper again (make sure the squares are true for templates - for drawing out this does not matter), and firm cardboard. Longer-lasting templates can be made of any material you can cut accurately such as transparent acetate and scraps of vinyl floor-covering.

Use of a paper-cutter
A guillotine, or paper-cutter, can be invaluable in cutting material for patchwork. A ruled grid on the plate will enable you to cut regular shapes quickly and accurately without templates. Needless to say, guillotines can be dangerous, and the type with a blade-guard is to be preferred.

PLANNING

When you plan a piece of patchwork, you must decide which block and which arrangement of it you prefer, how big the blocks are going to be and how many of them you will need to make.

WHICH BLOCK AND WHICH PATTERN?

Easy and difficult blocks

It is realistic to choose a block which you can sew without undue agonising. There should be pleasure in both the making and the contemplation of the finished product, and you will get little joy afterwards from a piece you did not enjoy making.

If you are experienced in sewing, you need not choose the easiest blocks and patterns, because you are used to handling a machine, and aspects like easing and matching are familiar to you. But if you have not sewn much by machine before, choose a block which counts as easy.

Easy blocks have fewer pieces, larger pieces, few or no diagonals, and less matching (of corners and straight lines). *Difficult* blocks have more pieces, smaller pieces, one or more diagonals and a lot of matching (eg of triangle points, or several points on each side as well as corners).

If you are a novice machine-user but want to use a block which counts as difficult, perhaps you can simplify it.
Consider these points :

> Can it be sewn with fewer pieces by making small changes?
> Can diagonal pieces be omitted?
> Can the amount of matching be reduced?

You may find that making one set of changes automatically solves other problems, in particular omitting diagonals, which reduces the number of pieces needed and usually results in less or less difficult matching.

3   Easy and more difficult block

4   Difficult block simplified

Patterns

Do not worry about whether a pattern is easy or difficult. Colour-changed or rotated blocks are no more difficult to piece than the original block; this needs only clear thinking and planning. Reflected blocks can be a complicating factor in a pattern, but again this is not a problem if you work it out carefully in advance.

The main point about patterns is to choose one you like. Blocks you like may not always yield patterns that please you.

Draw out possible patterns from the block (see Making Patterns, page 20). Use squared or isometric paper, and work in pencil; rule in block outlines before you start (with some patterns it is hard to keep track of block boundaries) and erase them when you have finished. Shade to indicate dark and light tones. You will have to draw at least nine blocks to get any impression of the overall pattern, and some arrangements will need 16 or 25 repeats for the eye to be able to read the pattern correctly.

To sum up, for early attempts at machine patchwork, choose a block and a pattern you like, and which you can piece and assemble in a relaxed way. Your first project should also be limited in scope : in practical terms, decide to make a cushion cover with nine blocks of three to six pieces each, rather than a double quilt of eighty blocks each with a dozen pieces.

WHAT SIZE OF BLOCK?

Remember that the larger the blocks, the fewer you need to make of them. If you halve the size of the block, it takes not twice but four times as many to cover the same area.

The general dimensions of the finished piece should be taken into consideration when you choose a block size. A large piece intended for a double bed can readily take a larger scale of pattern than a cushion or a small hanging. Traditional American quilts were often worked with a block size of 30 cm (12 in) and this (or larger) is a reasonable scale for a large project. Cot or crib quilts would be better with a smaller block, perhaps 20 cm (8 in) or even smaller. The size of the block should in any case be such that the overall pattern is clear to the eye : if the blocks are very large, there may not be enough repeats visible; if the blocks are too small, the effect may be lost in a blur.

Scaling up from block diagrams

The block diagrams, most of which are square, are based on a grid consisting of a number of units on

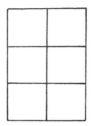 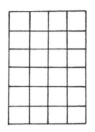

5   The same area is covered by six large and 24 small blocks

each side. You bring the block up to the size you want by deciding what measurement you want each unit to represent. Thus a 3 x 3 block will be 30 cm square if one unit represents 10 cm, or 6 in square if one unit is 2 in.

If you are using rectangular or diamond-shaped blocks (often on isometric paper), the principle is exactly the same : multiply each unit by a constant amount.

Tables 1a (metric) and 1b (imperial) show scaled up block sizes of square blocks of unit sizes 2 - 6.

TABLE 1a   SCALED-UP BLOCK SIZES (METRIC)

Block unit sizes are on the left, unit measurements in centimetres along the top. The body of the table shows the length in centimetres of one side of a square block. Sizes over 50 cm are omitted.

	2.5	4	5	6	8	10	12
2x2	5	8	10	12	16	20	24
3x3	7.5	12	15	18	24	30	36
4x4	10	16	20	24	32	40	48
5x5	12.5	20	25	30	40	50	
6x6	15	24	30	36	48		

TABLE 1b SCALED-UP BLOCK SIZES (IMPERIAL)

Block unit sizes are on the left, unit measurements in inches along the top. The body of the table shows the length in inches of one side of a square block. Sizes over 20 in are omitted.

	1	1½	2	2½	3	4	5
2x2	2	3	4	5	6	8	10
3x3	3	4½	6	7½	9	12	15
4x4	4	6	8	10	12	16	20
5x5	5	7½	10	12½	15	20	
6x6	6	9	12	15	18		

HOW MANY BLOCKS?

Working out how many blocks you need is first of all
a question of arithmetic, and later - if you want to
add borders - one of design. To help with calculations,
Tables 2a (metric) and 2b (imperial) give measurements for repeats of square blocks of various sizes.

TABLE 2a SIZE OF A NUMBER OF REPEATS (METRIC)

Block sizes in centimetres are on the left, numbers of
repeats along the top. The body of the table shows in
centimetres the size of a number of repeats. Sizes over
3 m are omitted.

	2	3	4	5	6	7	8	9	10	11	12	13	14	15
10	20	30	40	50	60	70	80	90	100	110	120	130	140	150
12	24	36	48	60	72	84	96	108	120	132	144	156	168	180
15	30	45	60	75	90	105	120	135	150	165	180	195	210	225
18	36	54	72	90	108	126	144	162	180	198	216	234	252	270
20	40	60	80	100	120	140	160	180	200	220	240	260	280	300
24	48	72	96	120	144	168	192	216	240	264	288			
30	60	90	120	150	180	210	240	270	300					
36	72	108	144	180	216	252	288							
40	80	120	160	200	240	280								

TABLE 2b SIZE OF A NUMBER OF REPEATS (IMPERIAL)

Block sizes in inches are on the left, numbers of repeats
along the top. The body of the table shows in inches
the size of a number of repeats. Sizes over 120 in are
omitted.

	2	3	4	5	6	7	8	9	10	11	12	13	14	15
4	8	12	16	20	24	28	32	36	40	44	48	52	56	60
5	10	15	20	25	30	35	40	45	50	55	60	65	70	75
6	12	18	24	30	36	42	48	54	60	66	72	78	84	90
8	16	24	32	40	48	56	64	72	80	88	96	104	112	120
10	20	30	40	50	60	70	80	90	100	110	120			
12	24	36	48	60	72	84	96	108	120					
15	30	45	60	75	90	105	120							
16	32	48	64	80	96	112								

Rectangular and diamond-shaped blocks

You can use the tables to work out how many rectangular blocks are needed to cover an area, calculating separately for each dimension.

A diamond block can be treated as a rectangle for purposes of calculation, as its area is the same as that of a related rectangle. Measure one side of the diamond; now measure straight across to the other side at right angles to the first line you measured. These two figures are used for further calculation as with rectangles. To assemble a rectangle from diamond blocks, you have to work in a special way (see *Diamond Assembly*, page 32).

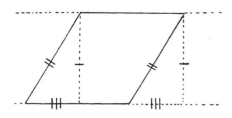

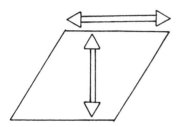

6 The measurements of the diamond block give the area of the rectangle

Using part-blocks

Because of the pattern

Sometimes the nature of the pattern formed by block repetition means you have to use part-blocks, for example where blocks are arranged like bricks in a wall. Here part-blocks, usually halves, occur at the ends of alternate rows.

To calculate how many part-blocks are needed, first work out the total as if you were using whole blocks throughout. Look at the pattern and note in how many rows part-blocks occur. Add this figure to your previous total to give you the number of blocks necessary. Note that you cannot just halve a whole block, because each half lacks a seam allowance along the cut edge.

You can assemble in two ways. Either use all the blocks with alternate rows staggered, and trim off the projecting part-blocks; or cut blocks (usually rectangular) from whole blocks, remembering to add a seam allowance, and assemble normally (diagram 7).

There are other patterns which need the addition of part-blocks to complete motifs and make the whole symmetrical. Thirds and quarters can be cut from opposite sides of whole blocks, which cuts the number you need to make by a few (diagram 8).

Observe that you again have to make extra blocks, parts of which are discarded. Experience shows that this is easier than making actual part-blocks, which may need new templates. Of course with some blocks it is very easy to make a part-block : any block with a vertical or horizontal seam all the way across permits this (diagram 9).

To reach a size

The other main case in which you need part-blocks is when you have to cover an area exactly with a block of a particular size.

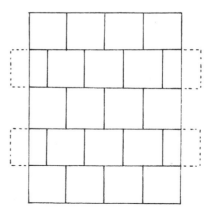

7 Trim projecting blocks straight

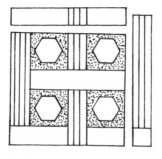

8 Part-blocks added to balance the pattern

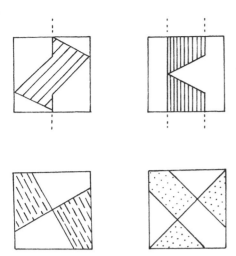

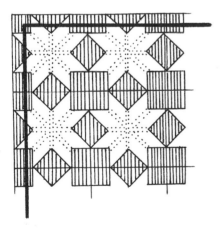

9 Above, easy half-block and quarter-block; others need new templates

Borders can be pieced from matching or toning material, and it is often a good idea to wait until the rest of the piece has been assembled before making final decisions about border colouring. It is also best to postpone a definite decision about the width — the eye should be able to judge which width is most appropriate to the rest of the piece.

Borders do not have to be plain. They can also be pieced in a design or pattern either related to the body of the patchwork or entirely different from it. Such borders can be of any width, up to block size or even wider. But if you want to make borders of whole blocks, choose blocks that make design sense when they appear as a single row. Some suitable border versions of blocks are suggested under *Block Designs*. A series of borders round a central area will give you the traditional framed or medallion patchwork often seen in quilts.

The easiest way of dealing with this is to assemble blocks into an area larger than you need, and trim to size evenly on all sides (diagram 10).

If you prefer you can work this out on paper first and decide which part-blocks you need. It is important for the pattern to be balanced, so often it is better to distribute a half block as a quarter on each side (eg make ¼ + 6 + ¼ blocks rather than 6 + ½).

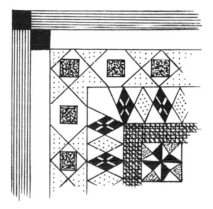

11 Pieced and plain borders framing the centre

10 Trim to size with an outer seam allowance

Borders
A simpler way to make an exact size, avoiding the use of part-blocks, is to add a border to the pieced area. Most pieces will have borders on all four sides, although bed coverings need no border at the top, where they are tucked in.

MAKING PATTERNS

Put together in a regular arrangement, blocks of more than one colour create repeat designs, or patterns. For any one block there are many different ways of doing this, more ways, perhaps, than one would guess. This section is an attempt to systematise various ways of deriving further patterns from the basic blocks given elsewhere. This systematisation allows you to try out different versions of a block in an orderly manner, and makes it possible to refer to patterns in words rather than diagrams.

COLOURING AND ROTATION

Colouring

The term colouring does not indicate the actual colours, but the relationship of dark and light tones in the block. In other words, a blue and white block is the same for this purpose as a green and yellow one - these are merely different realisations of the same dark/light design. But if you reverse the dark and light tones you get a new block, closely related to the original, but different. If the distribution of the tones is symmetrical, you get the same block a different way round (see *Rotation* below).

12   Blocks with colours reversed

Rotation or turning

Blocks can be symmetrical in different ways : vertically, horizontally and diagonally. If you take one half of the design and flip it over on the line or axis of symmetry, it matches the original second half. A block which is symmetrical in all three directions cannot be rotated or turned; whichever way up you put it, you are looking at the same design. But if there is any direction in which a block is not symmetrical, then you can rotate or turn it through 90°, 180° or 270°. Those who find geometry frightening can think of putting the block on its side

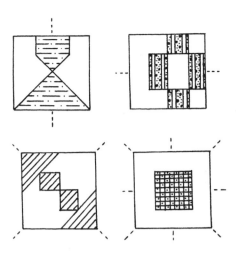

15 Four versions of a block

13 Lines of symmetry

or turning it upside down. You may say 'It's not really a new design, it's just the same one another way round', and of course you are right in this. But it is a standard method of making patterns, and what is interesting is the way changes of colouring and turning can be combined to create several patterns from a basic block.

Patterns from colour-changed and rotated blocks
This minimum of four designs can now be put together in different ways.

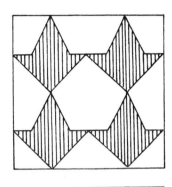

14 Blocks rotated

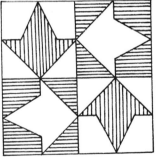

16 Patterns from the block (1 and 4 below)

Colour changes and rotation combined
Given that we are working with only two tones, light and dark, how can we combine colour changes and rotation?

Four or more designs can be derived from an block which has two tones and permits of turning : the basic block, the basic block with colours reversed, the basic block turned (up to three new positions, depending on symmetry) and the colour-reversed block turned (again possibly to more than one position).

(1) You can repeat the basic block every time.
(2) You can alternate in a chessboard pattern the basic block and the colour-changed block.
(3) You can alternate in a chessboard pattern the basic block and a turned block of the same colouring.
(4) You can alternate in a chessboard pattern the basic block and a turned block of opposite colouring.

21

Note that any of the derived designs can be combined, and that this does not need to be in a regular one-and-one chessboard alternation as above. Add the fact that many blocks permit of more than one turning, and you can see that the number of possible patterns is beginning to proliferate.

You may want to try out some patterns for yourself. Use squared paper, and draw in pencil. Using a ruler will make the outlines crisper and easier to read; you may prefer to shade in tones first and rule the outlines later. You need at least four repeats of block for the pattern to emerge, and nine repeats will be better.

If you make so many mistakes that you are wasting a lot of time, try instead drawing a number of separate blocks of each colouring. Make them a reasonable size (up to 10 cm/4 in), and use paper that is not too flimsy. Cut them out and move them round to see the effect. Physically manipulating blocks like this should help to make turning clear to you. Notice that you do not have to draw a turned block, you just turn it. If you find shading in large areas tedious, get a child to do it, or paint it in, or stick on newsprint for dark areas, leaving the others plain.

DROPPING AND SHIFTING

We have not yet exhausted the patterns that can be derived from a block. In the previous patterns the blocks are set together in straight lines vertically and horizontally. Instead of setting the blocks foursquare to each other, you can *drop* vertical rows, or *shift* horizontal rows.

When a block is dropped or shifted half the length of a side, this is called a half-drop or half-shift. It does not, however have to be a movement of a half; for 3x3 blocks it can (and probably more easily will) be a movement of one-third or two-thirds, ie one or two units out of three.

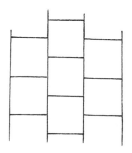
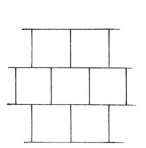

17 a Vertical rows dropped
   b Horizontal rows shifted

Patterns with repeated drops or shifts in the same direction often come out strongly diagonal. This can be changed into waves by regularly reversing the direction of the movement.

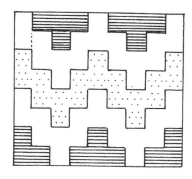

18   Rectangular block with the drop reversed to form waves

Dropping and shifting together
If you both drop and shift blocks, you create spaces between blocks, finishing with isolated motifs powdered on a background. You can sew this by incorporating the spaces into the original block.

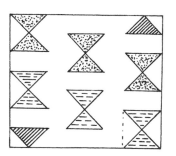

19   Blocks dropped and shifted; original 2 x 2 block and new 3 x 3 block

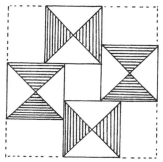
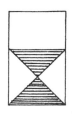

20   Drop plus shift round a square; rectangular block for filled out version

A combination of dropping and shifting can also produce a compact clustering of four blocks round a central square. The regular but many-sided figure formed can, perhaps contrary to expectations, be assembled by machine sewing, but it is not easy. This figure can be filled out with rectangles, restoring a square outline which can be assembled in the usual way. The special technique needed for sewing such a block is introduced on page 34.

REFLECTION

You may still be looking for a pattern you like. A further possibility is taking the reflection, or mirror-image, of a block

Take any block except a wholly symmetrical one, and add to its left or right its exact mirror image. Fill this out to a square by drawing underneath or above two more blocks mirroring the first two. You should now have a large symmetrical block the size of four

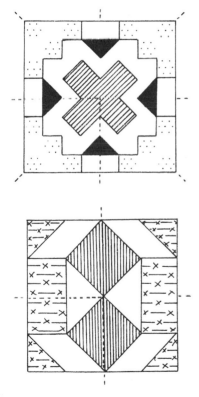

21   Reflected blocks, showing symmetry

original blocks. Observe that though you can reflect in different directions, right or left, up or down, and finish with apparently different large blocks, when

these are assembled, the same overall pattern will emerge, unless the blocks can be rotated.

The new large block can now be used in any way you like to try. Treat it as a basic block, and try colour changes, dropping and shifting. Some blocks will permit of turning, but further reflection produces nothing new.

MIXING

You can mix in whole blocks in one or more colours in a regularly alternating pattern. This is a good thing

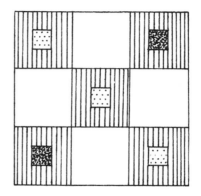

22   Alternating pattern

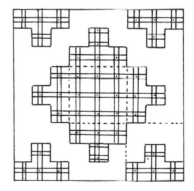

23   One plain and eight pieced blocks

to do if you are in a hurry to finish, because obviously it means you have to make many fewer pieced blocks.

COMBINING

You can combine two or more different blocks in a regular pattern. Try this first with blocks of the same unit size.

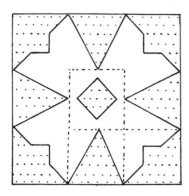

25 a   Alternate blocks turned

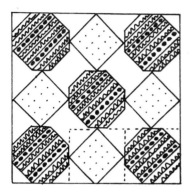

24   Combined patterns using more than one block

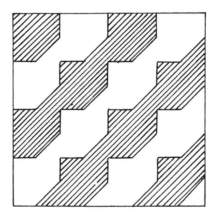

b   Alternate blocks colour-reversed

HOW MANY PATTERNS FROM ONE BLOCK?

It can easily be understood that the combination of all these operations on even a simple basic block allows a very large number of patterns to be derived. This means that however simple the block you have chosen, there is a choice of patterns available to you. So try drawing out a few alternatives before you commit yourself to a pattern, and remember that you can still experiment with rotation at a late stage when all the blocks have been completed.

For examples of the very different patterns that can be derived from a simple block (a square with one corner lopped off), see diagram 25. Four rows of four blocks make each pattern.

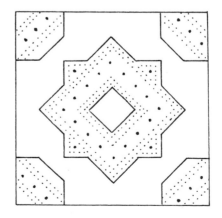

c   Reflection of 4 blocks from b

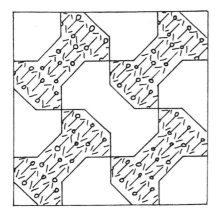

d   Colour change and rotation 1

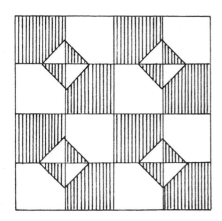

e   Colour change and rotation 2

f   Colour change and rotation 3

CUTTING AND SEWING

MAKING TEMPLATES

When you have chosen a block, the next step is to make templates so that you can cut out the material accurately. Each template will be the shape and size of a piece in the block, with added seam allowances.

Squared paper
You need squared paper. It does not matter what scale it is ie how big the squares are, provided they *are* square. Any paper where the squares are not true (eg from some school notebooks) can be kept for drawing out patterns, but for templates the paper must be exact. Some blocks need isometric paper; from now on, where squared paper is mentioned, it means paper with a ruled grid, squared or isometric as appropriate.

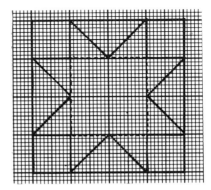

26   Block drawn out on squared paper

Draw out the block
Draw out the block, full size, on the paper. (See *Scaling up,* page 00). Use a ruler, and let horizontals and verticals fall directly on the ruled lines; diagonals of 45° should lie on the crossing lines of the grid. Keep this for reference.

Decide which templates you need
Instructions with Block Diagrams list the templates needed for a block, but for blocks you invent you must work it out. Look carefully at the block. Each different shape needs a template; however if a shape occurs in its mirror image, then you only need one template, which you flip over for the reflected pieces. If the pattern mixes in whole blocks of one colour, you also need a whole block template. Note that the number and variety of templates needed is a guide to whether the block is easy or difficult.

Draw out templates
Copy all templates exactly onto a fresh piece of paper, leaving wide margins round each. For simple blocks you can go directly to this stage without drawing a

complete block first. Use a sharp hard pencil, or a fine pen, to make all lines accurate and clear.

Decide on a seam allowance
Seam allowances will be 1 cm (3/8 in) or 1.25 cm (½ in) unless you are working with very small pieces or intend to quilt close to seams, when they can be 6-7 mm (¼ in). To decide the exact width, look at your paper : can you choose a seam width that will let you use the ruled lines? If so you will save time and can be assured of accuracy. You can draw in verticals and horizontals directly, but you will still have to measure diagonals.

Add seam allowances
Now add seam allowances to all template pieces. If you cannot use the lines of the grid, place a ruler or set square at right angles to a line and mark the width of the seam in several places. Connect these points to get the cutting line. Acute angles of triangles, diamonds etc will project, which is why the pieces had to be well spaced out. Be sure that the seam width is uniform for all pieces.

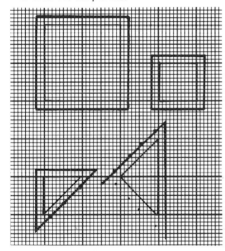

27 Templates with seam allowances

Stick pieces onto cardboard
Cut out each piece roughly, leaving the lines free. Glue each one onto medium-weight cardboard. Let them dry under a weight to make sure they are flat and even. Instead of cardboard you can use any other firm material that can be cut accurately.

Cut out templates
Work on a hard firm surface, protecting it if necessary with scrap cardboard or newspaper. Using for preference a craft knife laid along a ruler or straight edge, cut carefully on the outer (cutting) line. Edges can be taped to make the templates last longer. They are now ready for use.

Window templates
Window templates have a space in the middle corresponding to the final visible area of the sewn piece. They are useful for centring motifs if you want to use these in isolation, and for any pieces, like stripes, which need exact matching. You can also draw round the window to mark sewing lines; use a marker of which all traces will disappear, like chalk.

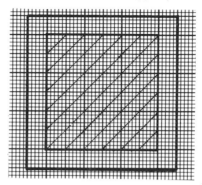

28 Window template (remove the shaded portion)

MARKING AND CUTTING OUT MATERIAL

Preparation of material
Materials for patchwork should be washed before use, to shrink them. If shrinkage occurs after pieces are sewn together, the work will wrinkle and pull instead of lying flat. Washing will also warn you of any dyes which are not fast, another obvious liability. Press materials immediately before cutting - crisp material makes cutting easier and faster.

Marking the material
Work on a flat hard surface. Outline templates on the back of the material. For regular shapes it does not make any difference which way up you have the template; but some angled pieces with diagonal edges are one-way, and templates for these must be laid face down, unless you want mirror image pieces.

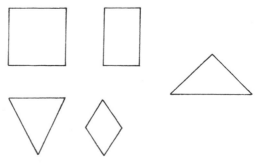

29 Shapes which are the same either way up

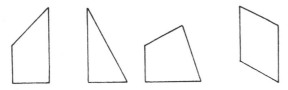

30 One-way shapes with different mirror images

Templates should be laid with their longer axis parallel to the selvages, with the grain. Sometimes you cannot do this, if for instance you are squeezing pieces from small scraps, or when a piece has to be cut on the cross or bias of the material for design reasons. But joining stretchy diagonal edges is never easy, so avoid it if possible. Try at least to place templates with their straight sides to a straight thread of the material.

Trace round the outside of the template with a pencil, a piece of chalk or soap - it must make a fine and distinct line tight along the edge of the template. Opinions are divided about the use of ball-point pens or fibre-tip markers. I have found that a quick light stroke with either is satisfactory, and prefer in this case to cut along the inside edge of the line so that few traces remain. With thin materials there is a risk that the line might show through, so exercise discretion. What matters is that the line must be clearly visible for cutting along, and marking must be done without pulling or stretching the material, which distorts the shape.

If the template slides around on the material, anchor it by roughening the side in contact. You can stick on sandpaper, felt or some coarsely-woven material like hessian (burlap). You could also lay a ruler along the template with its edge to the cutting line. This at once keeps the template in place and gives you a firm edge to draw along.

Each piece must be marked individually on a single thickness of material. Ideally there should be no common lines, to ensure that inaccuracies are not perpetuated.

Cutting out the material

Cut each side with a single stroke of the scissors, keeping tight to the line and neither wandering inside it nor diverging from it. I prefer to cut initially only enough pieces for one or two blocks, which I then assemble. This lets me check that templates and pieces are correct, and is a pleasing change of activity.

When you have finished cutting out, you can stack like pieces together, or sort out the pieces that belong to one block and keep them like that.

PUTTING A BLOCK TOGETHER

To assemble a block, the smallest pieces are first joined, then these in turn are added to larger pieces until the block is completed. Blocks are joined into strips or larger blocks, and these, sewn together, form the complete patchwork ready for finishing. This chapter deals with all stages up to finishing.

Machine

The machine should be set for straight stitching, with a medium stitch-length (about 4 sts/cm or 10 sts/in). Both top and bobbin threads should be of the same weight and quality, light or dark in colour as appropriate. It is easier to unpick if the thread shows up against the material.

Some machines are marked for seam widths on the plate to the right of the presser foot. If your machine is not marked, or you want to use a narrower width than is marked, you can mark for yourself. Lower the needle onto the sewing line of a template, and stick a piece of tape on the plate exactly at the edge of the template. Pieces are fed in with their raw edges exactly to this line, and the seam line is automatically in the right place.

Pieces

Sort out the pieces for one block, being careful to choose the right ones, specially if you are using any reflected pieces. You can lay out the pieces of a block in their positions, right side up, on the rough side of a piece of hardboard (masonite). (I also use the smooth side for leaning on when tracing outlines and cutting out templates).

Piecing (joining)

Remember that you are always joining adjacent pieces — the laid out block will help with this. Put your first two pieces right side to right side matching the seam lines. (See also *Placing* below.)

Now sew the seam, keeping the edges of the pieces exactly on the marked line. Try not to sew too slowly; if you have to stop halfway, be sure the needle is in its lowest position, otherwise there will be a 'step' in the middle. The ends of thread need not be trimmed close, because they will all be underneath and will not show. You do not have to tie them, or backstitch, because every seam will be locked by being crossed by another seam.

There is no need to tack or pin pieces before sewing, although you can do this if you wish. Use rustless pins, and check that they do not mark the material. Pin perpendicular to the sewing line, and remove the pins as soon as possible.

Placing pieces

With pieces like squares and rectangles, matching the seam lines automatically gives matched edges and corners. But this is not the case with any piece which has a diagonal edge : angles and points project, and it may be hard to see how to position such angled pieces for sewing.

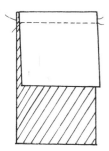

31   Joining right angles : corners and edges match

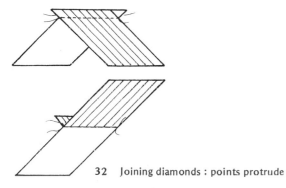

32   Joining diamonds : points protrude

Diamonds need care. Think of what you do when you join bias strips of material : you place them so that a narrow angle projects on each side. If you matched the raw edges, the long sides would come out wrong.

For other angled pieces, go back to your templates, and observe where the sewing line lies. Trace the templates onto thin or transparent paper, with sewing lines marked. Now hold the papers right side to right side, and align the sewing lines exactly, holding the papers up to the light so that you can see the lines clearly. Pin or stick the papers together, and this will give the right alignment for the material pieces.

Pressing

All seams benefit from being pressed before they are crossed by other seams in subsequent joining. Seams should be pressed flat, not open. Whenever you press a seam, you have to make a decision about the direction. In general you want to press so that seam thicknesses are distributed — many machines balk at suddenly being asked to sew through several thick-

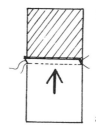

33   Pressing :
a   Towards dark piece
b   For later quilting of octagon
c   Meeting seams lie in opposite
    directions

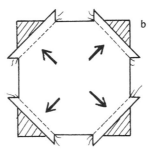

nesses. Pressing just before further joining should help; then you can tell which way seams should fall for easy machining. The following are some points to bear in mind. Seams joining light to dark materials should be pressed to fall to the dark side (they can show through light colours). Press away from where any quilting stitches will be (you do not want extra layers to stitch through). Seams which meet should be pressed to fall on opposite sides.

Pressing a seam back on itself takes up a fractional amount of material. Small infelicities may therefore be improved or corrected by pressing so that the piece which is too short or too small lies flat.

Very occasionally a seam can be pressed open. This might be to prevent the build-up of too many thick-nesses — where eight points of a star meet, for example. You can also press seams open in very small pieces of work, where flat seams seem to show more.

It is usual to press from the front, but have a look at the back first, so that you can sort out any crossed seams — where a seam sewn down at both ends faces up at one end and down at the other. Here the thing to do is snip into the right angle at one side, permitting the rest of the seam to lie the way it wants. Finish by pressing firmly from the front, at a temperature app-ropriate to the most sensitive of your materials.

If you do not have a steam iron, you can make steam by spraying lightly first, or by pressing over a damp-ened cloth. Steam gives crisp seams, and flattens tiny puckers.

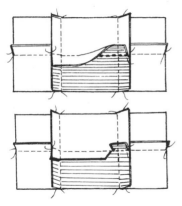

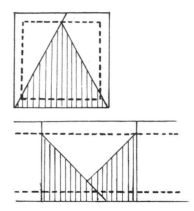

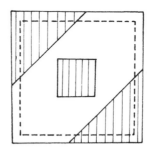

36 Floating triangle points (assembly seams touch the top points)

34 Correcting crossed seams

Final stages of assembling a block

When all the small pieces have been joined, assemble them with each other and/or larger pieces to make the block.

Matching

The most important aspect of this stage is matching. You may have to join two pieced areas to give a quartered effect. Pin pieces together with the joins matching exactly. It is now more important to match points and seams than edges, so the outside edges may no longer be level. Small deviations can be expected and will still permit proper assembly, but serious shortfalls will create problems later.

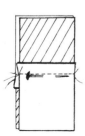

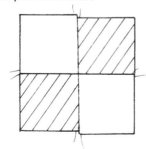

37 The dotted assembly seam shows the finished size

35 Match the seams not the edges of the pieces

At some point you will probably notice that shapes like triangles appear to have their points floating on their own. Do not worry, this is as it should be. Further joining will take up the seam allowances on the outside of the points, letting them reach the edge of the block.

Looking at a whole block

The completed single block is bigger than the full-size drawn out block by the amount of the seam allowance on all sides. Do not let this disturb you.

Some patterns include single colour blocks of whole block size. Looking at the pieced blocks which should

accompany them, you may find that the pieced blocks are slightly smaller. This happens above all when there are a lot of pieces and several interior seams in the pieced block. Seams do take up some material. There are two things you can do to cope with this : trim the plain blocks by a fraction, or use a slightly reduced seam allowance when joining the pieced blocks. (This only works if the pattern permits — it is no answer if lines that should reach the edge of the block fail to do so.)

Assembly-line

Once you are sure how a block is put together, you can work on an assembly-line basis, joining all the like pieces for a number of blocks before going on to the next stage for all blocks. This is a good method for handling awkward positioning of pieces : work it out and then join them all while placement is fresh in your mind.

You can also save time by running pairs of pieces through the machine without cutting the threads between them. Pull each pair out behind the presser foot to free the threads for the next pair. Even faster is feeding pairs in very close on one another, watching that you do not attach them. However some

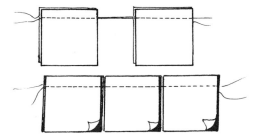

38 Joining without cutting threads between pieces

machines object to making even a single stitch without material under the foot, and when you detach pieces, the closely-cut ends of thread may allow a couple of stitches to come undone. Either way, you finish with a string of pieces, which can stay attached till you come to the next stage, when you snip them off one by one.

It should be stressed that you should not set up an assembly-line until you are certain that you are putting the block together correctly. Refer back often to a sample block; the repetitive nature of what you are doing can easily persuade you that something is right when it is not.

ASSEMBLY

There are two ways you can join blocks : in strips, and in larger blocks. No instructions are given for a lattice set or assembly, where blocks are divided from each other by strips of material. This is because many of the patterns given take their effect from immediate juxtaposition.

Strips

Make sure you know how many blocks you want to put together in each direction, and that the total number of blocks is correct. Now begin to join adjacent sides of blocks into strips, always checking that you are joining the intended sides of blocks. Pin first, matching points and corners as necessary. The width of the seam allowance is now a secondary factor, provided it does not fall below 6-7 mm (¼ in), so you can weave around between corners in favour of matching. Continue joining blocks until the right number are joined. Shorter lengths are slightly easier to handle : to join 8 x 6 blocks I prefer eight strips of six to six strips of eight.

When all the strips have been assembled, they themselves can be joined — the most difficult of matching problems. Pin matching points or corners as before : you can tack or baste if you think it is easier. You may be able to aid matching by resewing seams or

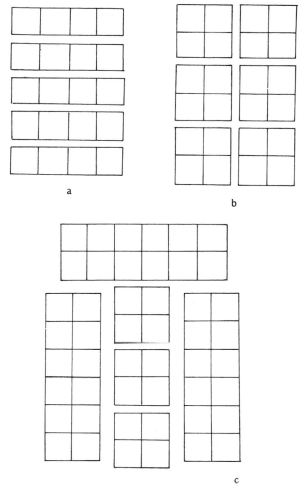

39 Assembly : a   In strips
b   In blocks
c   In fours working outwards

part-seams in the strips, taking up or letting out by a fraction. Be careful that the weight and bulk of the piece do not divert you too far from the intended placement of seams.

Strip assembly of random work

Lay out your whole set of blocks to find the best arrangement to avoid unhappy runs of clashing colours or touching blocks of like colouring. Stack rows all in the same direction, pinning a number to the top block of each row; this stays in place until assembly is complete.

Blocks

Assembly in blocks means joining blocks in fours or nines, and then sewing these together in fat strips or by working out from the centre. Some patterns are easier to assemble in this way than in strips.

Assembling diamonds

You can work out how many diamonds cover a particular rectangular area (page 18). These are assembled in vertical or diagonal strips, or even in larger diamonds. But when you join the strips with the tops in a line, you have a large diamond, not a rectangle. This can easily be converted into a rectangle of the same height and width (or in certain cases a square).

Lay the large diamond lengthways on the floor, face up. Mark horizontally across the width from the bottom left angle of the diamond to a point on the opposite side; this line should be at right angles to both sides. Cut across the line to give you a separate right-angled triangle. Now join the long side of this triangle to the diagonal running from the top left of the original diamond. This final seam is always diagonal, however you originally assembled. The diamond is now a rectangle of the right dimensions. This is a much easier way of working than calculating with and sewing a number of part-diamonds.

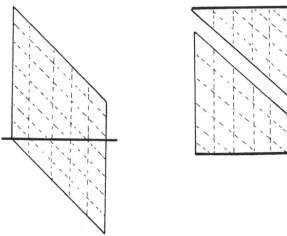

41   Converting a diamond to a rectangle

Adding borders

Borders are added after the blocks have been assembled. Measure the width of the piece. Cut or piece long rectangular border pieces for one or both ends as required; their width can be decided now, by eye, if you do not have to make an exact finished size. Seam the borders to the patchwork. Now measure again, this time the entire length of the patchwork plus added borders. Cut or piece long rectangles of this length, with the width as decided. Seam these to the long sides of the work. The corners can be mitred (see books on sewing technique for this).

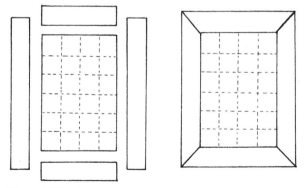

42 a   Adding border strips
   b   Border with mitred corners

The plain or one-colour border is the simplest kind of border. Pieced borders are added last in the same way. Turning corners can be a problem, as you can see if you look at photographs in books on the history of patchwork. So choose a size for a border block which will let you urn the corners easily. You may even have to invent a block to carry pattern lines round corners. Another solution is simply to make the corner block a plain one.

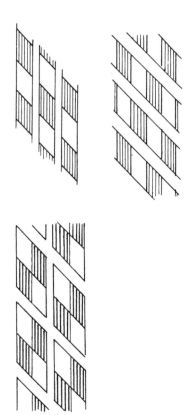

40   Diamond assembly : vertical and diagonal strips, large
      diamonds

SPECIAL TECHNIQUES

SEW AND CUT

Normally when making patchwork you cut out the pieces and then join them. There are times, however, when it is possible, and much easier, to sew first and then cut to size. It is faster as well as easier to join two strips with a single long seam than to sew several short seams, even if they add up to the same length.

This method is suitable for certain types of blocks. It can be used both where pieces of the same size and shape are to be joined and where they are neither the same size nor shape.

a   b

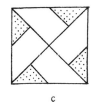

43   Block *a*, Block *b*, Block *c*

c

You start by cutting or tearing strips which are the finished width plus twice the seam allowance. Tearing is easier, but does not work well with any printed pattern that fails to lie straight to the grain of the material, unless it is a small scale print where this is not obvious. The strips can be of any convenient length depending on the material.

For Block *a* you need two strips, one of light and one of dark; the horizontal rows in Block *b* need three strips, arranged dark/light/dark for top and bottom rows, and light/dark/light for the middle row. The strips are joined with the normal seam allowance.

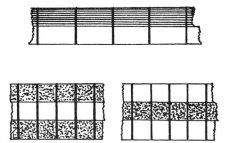

44   Joined strips for Blocks *a* and *b*; cutting lines marked

Now you need templates to mark the strips for cutting. Block *a* needs a 2 x 2 template, Block *b* a 3 x 1 template (in each case plus seam allowances). Mark the strips and cut them.

For Block *c* draw out the triangle and measure it to find the right width for the strips. Join strips as before, and make a new template, a triangle which is a diagonal quarter of the block (add seam

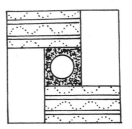

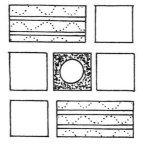

47   Normal piecing of the block

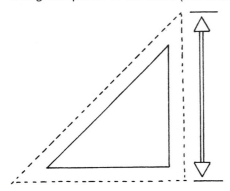

45   Width of the dark strip

allowances). For a simple repeat of the block, cut all triangles the same way; other triangles of opposite colouring will be left over. You can use both versions if your pattern also needs colour-changed blocks. Be careful with the placement of the template so that you get the right triangles.

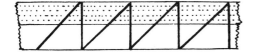

46   Joined strips for Block *c*; cutting lines marked

In all cases where you cut triangular shapes from strips, their long sides will be on the cross of the material (as they probably would be anyway if you cut them separately). You need to be careful that the material is not stretched when such edges are being joined. Also remember not to pull joined seams about — the stitching, being cut close, may easily come undone. It is a good idea to use a slightly shorter stitch length for sewing strips together.

HALF OPEN SEAMS

With most machine patchwork you are looking for straight seams to join. Setting-in, for example of L-shaped pieces, is generally handled by adding an extra join. But sometimes you can sew what appears to be an L-shape without having to piece in this way.

Consider a block consisting of four rectangles grouped about a central square. Put another way, the lines of the square are continued to the edges of the block, and this fact is the clue to assembly.

To sew the block in the normal way with piecing you join seven pieces in three rows, two of the outer rectangles having central joins. But it can also be sewn in the following way.
(1) Join 1 and 2, from a point half way down the side of 1 to the junction with 3.
(2) Join 3 to 1 − 2.

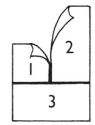

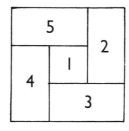

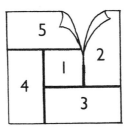

48   Piecing with half open seams

(3) Join 4 to 1 − 3.
(4) Join 5 to 4 − 1, turning down the top of 2 to keep it out of the way.
(5) Fold over 2 and complete the half seam with which you began.

You may have to snip into the angle of 1, 2 and 3 to allow access. Start in the middle, where 1 and 2 meet, and overrun the previous seam by a few stitches, keeping exactly on the line. Sew to the edge of the block.

You have now made the same block with fewer pieces and no interior seams in the rectangles.

Another use of the same technique of half open seams is to make a 'one-patch' rectangle pattern with stepped joins, a pattern familiar to most of us from parquet flooring. Although not a block, this pattern appears in the *Block diagrams* section, where exact instructions are given. Briefly, the pieces are joined in V-shaped diagonal strips, with the outside seam always left half open; the strips are then assembled, starting from the other end and completing all the half seams.

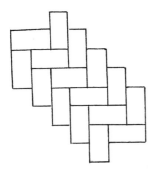

49 a   Parquet pattern

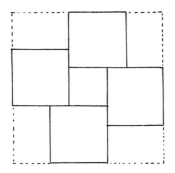

b   Filled-out drop plus shift

The half open seam technique is useful in a number of blocks, which are grouped together in the *Block diagrams*, and for the parquet pattern. It must also be

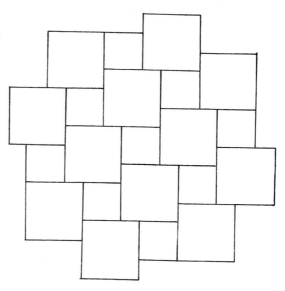

50   Overall drop plus shift

used if you want to make a pattern from four blocks joined with drop plus shift. The easiest version of this is with the block filled out to a square by the addition of four rectangles. First join the rectangles to the squares, then, starting and finishing with a half open seam, join these around the small central square.

It is also possible to use the half open seam technique to assemble an overall drop plus shift pattern. Assembly works on the same principle as the parquet pattern — almost all seams are left half open until finally joined. Make a sample before you start on a project of this kind; and if you are wise, your first project at least will be limited in size.

PROBLEMS

On these pages a number of possible problems — which can arise even with the closest of attention — are brought together, and some solutions and consolation offered. Some of the points have been touched on before, but it seems useful to bring them together under one heading for ease of reference. The problems are roughly ordered from initial stages to assembly, and exclude difficulties relating to finishing.

I can't get graph paper/isometric paper
On pages 143 and 144 you will find large and small scale squared and isometric grids. Use tracing paper laid over the small scale pages (secure it with paper clips) to draw out designs and patterns. The large scale pages are for tracing off templates.

I can't sew straight on a machine
There are two possibilities here : either you genuinely find it difficult, or the machine is at fault. Look at your machine first. Is the needle pulling to one side because it is bent? Is the tension even? Are the top and bottom threads the same? Is there a lot of fluff around the bobbin case? Any of these could make it more difficult to sew straight clean seams. Check the instruction book for how to feed in material — you may be pulling it to one side. Perhaps you are letting the ends of the seams slide around. With small pieces of material which you may be holding too tight it is easy to let the seam line slide to the right at the end of a seam, so that the stitching falls within the seam allowance, and the piece is wider at one end than the other.

You might feel better and more cofident if you had a line to sew along. In that case make window templates, and mark the pieces from them. It is not actually all that much easier to sew straight along a line, as you will find out if you try with a piece of ruled paper. But having a line will free your attention from the edges of the material and let you concentrate on the stitching line. Remember if you are using window templates that you only see half the lines you draw (the others are out of sight underneath) so it is a big effort to make by the time you have drawn in lines on every single piece.

The thread keeps breaking
Check your machine as above, specially the tension, but only after you have looked at the thread you are using. If it is of poor quality, with knots or snags, it will break every time one of those has to pass through a narrow space. Use good quality thread, for preference new, as cotton dries out and becomes brittle with age.

The pieces don't fit together

Check every stage, scaling-up, drawing out, making templates, cutting out, choice and arrangement of pieces, with particular attention to mirror-image pieces if they occur. If all of these are right, then the chances are that the pieces do in fact fit together, and your difficulty is seeing how they do so. Go back to your templates and consider how the seam lines ought to lie. Sometimes you have to go ahead on trust. I have often frankly disbelieved that particular pieces would ever form a promised design or pattern, but usually they have come together in the end. One of my problems is inadvertently using a piece the wrong way up, specially when it is cut from material which has no obvious right or wrong side.

I can't match the points

Nobody has difficulty in matching points on squared paper, so the answer must be that the pieces are inaccurate in size. Check all stages, including the width of the seam allowance — it is possible that you have joined with a dressmaking seam width if you have been sewing clothes on your machine recently. Look at the material of which the pieces are made — perhaps it has stretched in the sewing, and that is why matching is hard.

The seams are all twisting at the back

Let them lie the way they want to by snipping diagonally into a right angle at one end of the twisting seam. Then the rest of the seam can lie flat the other way.

It's going to come out too big

Check your scaling up measurements. You may have tripled or quadrupled when you meant to double a figure. Otherwise, remember that the smaller the pieces, the wider the seam allowance is in proportion. A 2.5 cm (1 in) square will be at least half as big again with its seam allowances, whereas a 25 cm (10 in) measurement is only a little longer on all sides. It is tempting to lay out the pieces of block with their edges touching, and this can give you a totally false impression of how big it will be.

The block is much more difficult than I thought

Sewing an early block will help you spot the difficultie. You could leave this particular block until you are more experienced; you could abandon the project and use the material for another simpler block. You can also go on. Often a difficult block will sort itself out with repetition, and it is worth persevering, specially if your main difficulties were working out things like placement, and you took a long time over the block. If the block is a total disaster, give in, and give it up. At least you have not wasted much material.

The edges of the blocks don't match

Minor mismatching is almost so common as to be expected. Major failure to match must be remedied by surgery, ie by making replacement blocks. Minor failure is handled by lengthening or shortening by unpicking and resewing either internal block seams or block joining seams; or else by joining with a slightly larger or smaller seam allowance than usual.

One block is far too small

This is an exaggerated version of the last problem. The only satisfactory answer is to make a replacement block, as there is clearly no way a block can fill a space if it has nothing over for seam allowances. As long as you have at least 6 mm (¼ in) available for the seams, the block can be used, no matter what the seam allowance ought to be. With less than this, it really is not worth trying.

I've run out of material on the 78th block

Find another material of similar tone values — this is more important than an exact colour match. Should you need a small blue floral pattern, look for a green or purple print of similar scale and tone instead of hoping to use blue checks or stripes. You might also be able to piece from the remaining scraps of the original material. Quite narrow strips can be joined and pressed; you can then cut from the template. Or half pieces can be cut, allowing for a joining seam, and assembled. With a small print, such internal seams will hardly show.

The fourth block in row five is upside down

If your patchwork is finished, backed, quilted or mounted, then there is nothing you can do but invite your family and friends to spot the error. You will be consoled by the fact that very few people will find it immediately.

If the patchwork is assembled but not finished, the problem can be remedied. Carefully unpick the seams around that block, and resew with it correctly positioned. There is no need to undo whole seams across the width or the length of the piece.

I've finished my project, but I don't like it

This happens to all of us sometimes. Find a worthy recipient — this might be somebody running a raffle or lottery for a school or church fair or bazaar. With luck, you won't win it back. Whoever wins it will probably be thrilled.

But before you get rid of it, consider honestly why you do not like it, and what went wrong between your initial choice and completion. It may be the colours or the materials; it may be some overall pattern you do not like that only became clear as you assembled; perhaps finishing gave you trouble, or you were in such a hurry to finish that you rushed and did not stop to put mistakes right. Try to identify the cause of your disenchantment, so that you can learn from what have turned out to be mistakes, and can start to plan your next project with enthusiasm and confidence.

Parenthetically, I have to confess here that it took over 2000 hand-sewn hexagons in random colours to convince me of the virtues of pre-planning pattern and colour.

BLOCK DESIGNS

INTRODUCTION

The 40 block designs which follow are arranged in several groups :

1 — 10   Blocks using squares and rectangles only, no diagonals; sew and cut technique is used.

11 — 14   Blocks including diagonals for which sew and cut can be used.

15 — 20   Blocks illustrating and using half open seam technique (not necessarily more difficult than other blocks).

21 — 28   Isometric blocks (ie drawn on isometric paper) including hexagon shapes and 60° angles. Some blocks are diamond-shaped, but are no more difficult than square blocks.

29 — 40   These include more difficult blocks and patterns, and some using two blocks which may be of different sizes. Others are blocks which do not readily fall into any other category.

To use the Block Designs

Scale up the block to the desired size (page 16). Remember that the blocks illustrate the final sewn size and that *they do not include* seam allowances — you always have to add these.

Layout

A version of each pattern is illustrated sewn (to prove it can be done) and drawn out with one block (occasionally two) indicated in heavy lines. Then a single block is shown, to clarify unit size; and an 'exploded' version of the block shows how it is put together. Note that some pieces are shown already joined, meaning that you can use the sew and cut method if you want. Like the single block diagrams, exploded blocks show completed sewn sizes of pieces, and take no account of seam allowances; they are meant as a guide to placement of pieces for assembly and not as a blueprint for sizes.

For each basic block (ie not for variations of colour or turning) the following information is given :

(1) the *unit size* of the block and the total number of pieces (+ 1 means you also need a complete whole block)

(2) which *templates* are needed (where possible this is stated in terms of units, eg 2 x 1 rectangle, 3 x 3 square; 1 x 1 triangle means a diagonally halved 1 x 1 square)

(3) how many *pieces* of each tone go to make one block

(4) how to *piece* and *assemble* blocks

(5) *comments* on suitability for random colouring using a variety of scraps; and on further patterns derived from the block, or from modifications of it.

Abbreviations	
D	dark tone
L	light tone
C or C 1	contrast tone ie third colour
C 2, C 3	further contrast tones
SA	seam allowance

BLOCK DESIGN 1

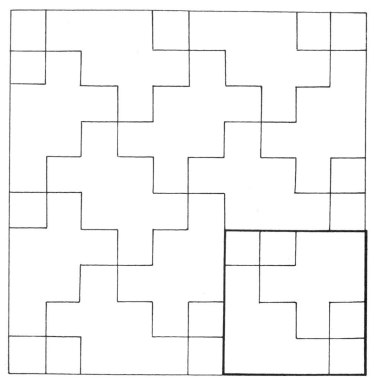

51   Block 1 pattern

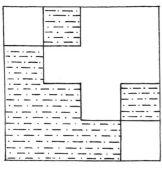

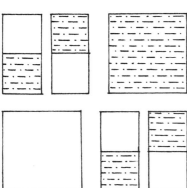

52 4 x 4 block, 10 pieces

Templates
2 x 2 square, 1 x 1 square
(2 x 1 rectangle for sew and cut method)

Cutting
D one large square, four small squares
L one large square, four small squares

Piecing
Join small squares in pairs, or use sew and cut.
Matching centre seams, make up quarter blocks.
Join on large squares on correct sides and complete
the block by joining the halves, matching centre seams.

Assembly
Assemble in strips, matching corners and mid-block
seams carefully.

Comments
The jagged weave pattern only appears when several
blocks have been put together. Use the same two
tones throughout.

53 Alternative block (11 pieces)

Use the alternative block for random colouring of one
tone; here an entire figure appears in one block,
which aids planning. Each figure can be a different
colour, but keep up a firm contrast with the background tone.

Plain blocks can be alternated, with every second row
of pieced blocks turned to break up the strong
diagonal effect.

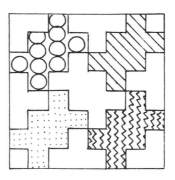

54 a Scrap colouring

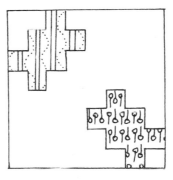

b Turned, with alternate plain blocks

BLOCK DESIGN 2

55 Block 2 pattern

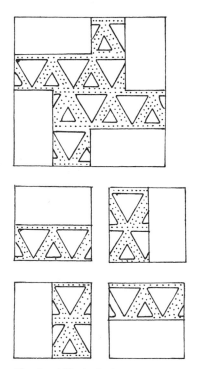

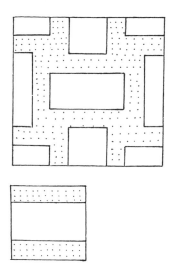

57   Reflected pattern and alternative block

56   4 x 4 block, 8 pieces

Templates
2 x 1 rectangle
(2 x 2 square for sew and cut method)

Cutting
D four rectangles
L four rectangles

Piecing
Join pairs of D and L rectangle to make quarter
blocks. Watch the positioning when you join these
into halves (the stripes in adjacent pieces are always
at right angles, with D in the centre). Joining the two
halves completes the block.

Assembly
Assemble in strips or blocks, always matching the
sides of the blocks; corners bring like colours together
and so are less important.

Comments
You can easily use random colours for the cross in
each block, keeping the other tone the same.

Reflection gives a new allover pattern of rectangles.
Depending on the colouring scheme chosen, this
could also be sewn with a simple alternative block. It
is always a good idea to look at a derived pattern for
a possible simpler block.

BLOCK DESIGN 3

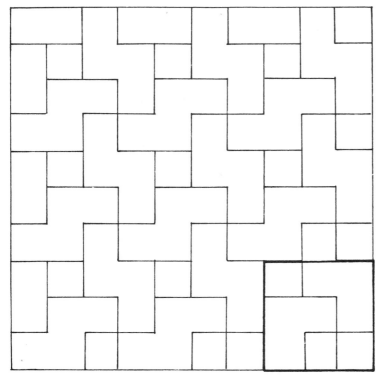

58 Block 3 pattern

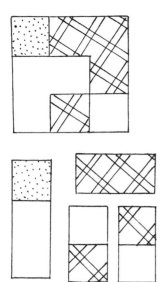

with half drop or shift relieves the squareness of the pattern. Quite suitable for scrap use, the block is pieced in four quarters with careful matching of the centre.

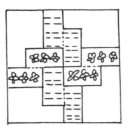

61   6 x 6 stepped cross

59   3 x 3 block, 7 pieces

Templates
2 x 1 rectangle, 1 x 1 square
(3 x 1 rectangle for sew and cut method)

Cutting
D one rectangle, two squares
L one rectangle, two squares
C one square

Piecing
Join as shown, matching as necessary. Use sew and cut if you want.

Assembly
Assemble in strips or blocks, matching corners and sides. You can add an extra 1/3 block to complete the dark motifs at the top, leaving off 1/3 block at the bottom for the same reason, but it is impossible to complete step shapes of both tones.

Comments
One motif extends over two blocks, so this is not an easy pattern for random colouring.

A 6 x 6 block is formed by using four motifs to make a stepped cross on a background. Repetition of this

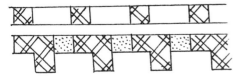

60   Adding to complete motifs

BLOCK DESIGN 4

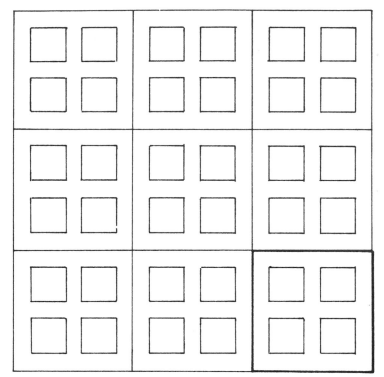

62 Block 4 pattern

46

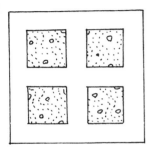

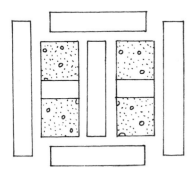

63 7 x 7 block, 11 pieces

Templates
2 x 2 square, rectangles 2 x 1, 5 x 1 and 7 x l

Cutting (L block)
D four squares
L two small, three mid and
two large rectangles.

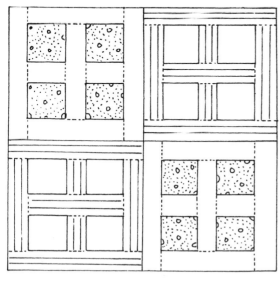

64 Assemble turning D blocks

Piecing
Sew and cut saves a lot of time. Use the 5 x 1 templates to cut up the strips. Join vertical strips of three
pieces on either side of the central rectangle, then add
top, bottom and finally side rectangles. Always work
out from the centre.

Assembly
Cutting instructions are for a L block (ie light frame);
alternate L and D blocks make up the pattern. Match
corners and assemble in blocks or strips, turning all
blocks of one colouring so that the long edge pieces
of adjacent blocks run in different directions.

Comments
This block is ideal for the use of scraps, provided D
and L tones can clearly be distinguished — otherwise
the pattern is lost.

BLOCK DESIGN 5

65   Block 5 pattern

48

Block Design 16

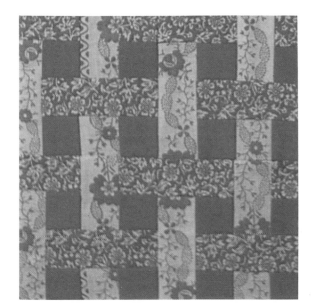

Block Design 23

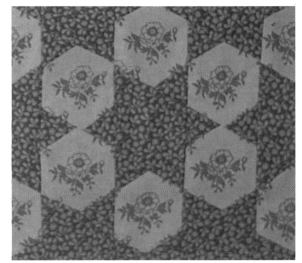

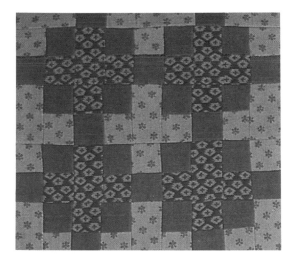

Block Design 6

Block Design 37

Cushion: Block Design 14

Bath mat: Block Design 33

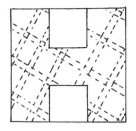

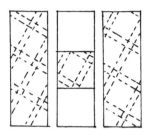

66   3 x 3 block, 5 pieces

The H-shape can be manipulated to produce further interesting patterns, for instance four blocks in a filled-out drop plus shift arrangement (join into large square using a half open seam).

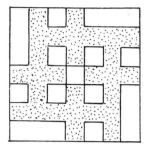

68   Filled-out drop plus shift

Templates
3 x 1 rectangle, 1 x 1 square

Cutting (D block)
D two rectangles, one square
L two squares

Piecing
The 3 x 1 template is used to cut from strips in the sew and cut method. Make D and L blocks.

Assembly
Assemble in strips of alternate D blocks and turned L blocks, starting strips with D and L in turn. Assembly into blocks of four might be easier. Corners must be matched, and block seams should run in exact verticals and horizontals. Add 1/3 blocks at sides to complete D motifs.

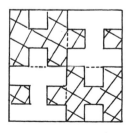

67   Assembly in fours

Comments
This is suitable for scraps if one tone is kept constant. Because the figures run over three blocks, it is easiest to assemble in vertical strips, using one material as L in an entire vertical strip.

BLOCK DESIGN 6

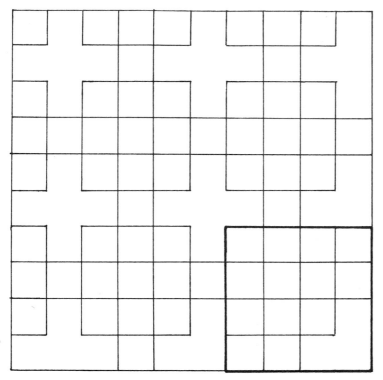

69   Block 6 pattern

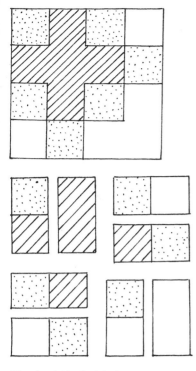

Piecing
Various versions of sew and cut can be tried, but avoid any method which finishes with several whole block seams running in the same direction. Join pieces in threes and fours to form quarter blocks, and match centre and seams when joining these.

Assembly
Assemble in strips or blocks, with attention to all matching. Add extra quarter blocks at top and left to complete the pattern.

Comments
The dark crosses can easily be coloured at random.

A simpler pattern using an easier block is made by omitting the D crosses altogether and working in two tones only.

70 4 x 4 block, 14 pieces

Templates
2 x 1 rectangle, 1 x 1 square

Cutting
D one rectangle, three squares
L one rectangle, three squares
C six squares

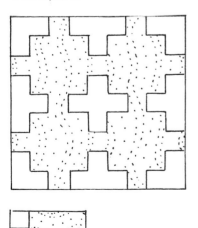

71 Pattern from easier block

BLOCK DESIGN 7

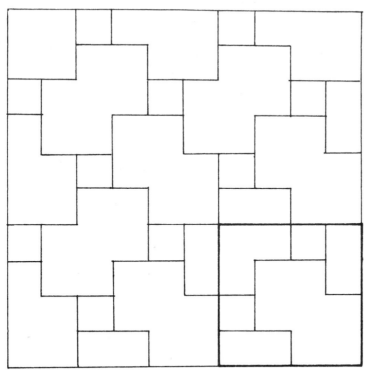

72   Block 7 pattern

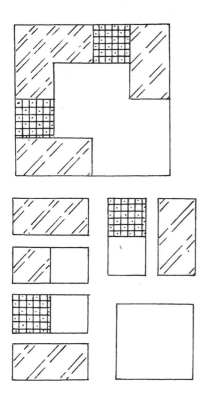

Piecing
Using sew and cut method if you want, join pieces to form quarter blocks and assemble them to complete the block, matching as necessary.

Assembly
Assemble in blocks or strips, matching centres of block sides. Add or omit a quarter block at right and bottom to balance the pattern.

Comments
A whole L figure occurs in a block, so these could be pieced from scraps of different colours, provided the D/L contrast is maintained.

The pattern is also attractive set on the diagonal.

73   4 x 4 block, 10 pieces

Templates
2 x 2 square, 2 x 1 rectangle, 1 x 1 square

Cutting
D three rectangles, one small square
L one large square, three small squares
C two small squares

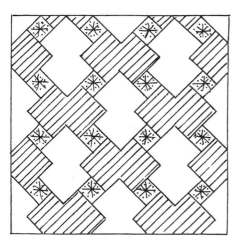

74   Pattern set on diagonal

BLOCK DESIGN 8

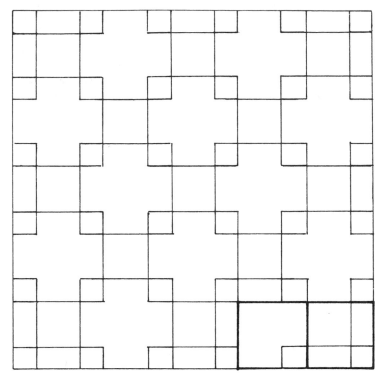

75 Block 8 pattern

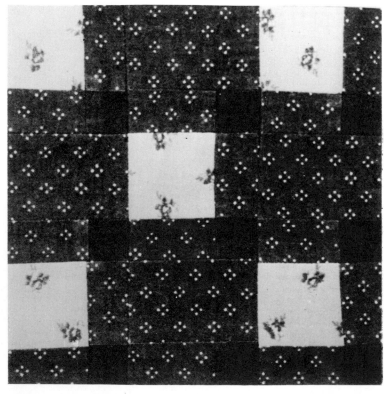

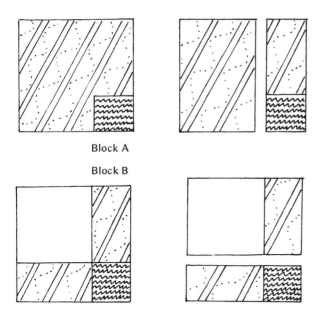

Block A

Block B

76 3 x 3 blocks; Block A : 3 pieces, Block B : 4 pieces

Templates
2 x 3 rectangle, 2 x 2 square, 2 x 1 rectangle, 1 x 1 square

Cutting
Block A : D one large rectangle, one small rectangle
            C one small square
Block B : D two small rectangles
            L one large square
            C one small square

Piecing
Use sew and cut if you want. Match seams in Block B.

Assembly
Blocks A and B alternate throughout. Assemble in strips or blocks, whichever is easier for the matching of block sides, which must be exact for the effect. Add 1/3 of a block at top and left to complete the pattern.

Comments
As the pattern is one of overlapping squares, C pieces can conveniently be a darker tone of whatever colour you use for D. You could of course also overlap two different colours and choose an appropriate C tone. For this you would need a full plan in colour for close reference at every stage.

BLOCK DESIGN 9

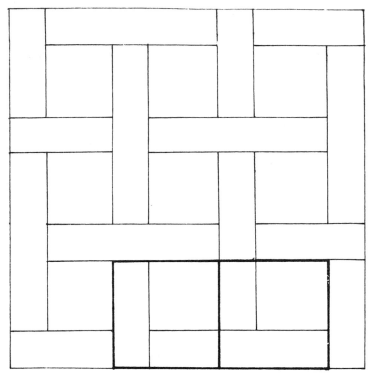

77　Block 9 pattern

79 Adding quarter blocks

Assembly

Assemble in strips or blocks according to how easy
you find the exact matching of corners and block
sides, alternating the blocks. Balance the pattern by
adding quarters at top and right, or omitting them at
bottom and left.

Comments

This is one way of producing a weave effect. Colouring should remain the same for D and L throughout,
though scraps could be used for the squares. Use a
window template to ensure exact centring if you
want to have isolated motifs in the squares.

78 4 x 4 block, 3 pieces

Templates

3 x 3 square, 3 x 1 and 4 x 1 rectangles (3 x 4
rectangle for sew and cut method)

Cutting

D 3 x 1 rectangle ⎱
L 4 x 1 rectangle ⎰ reverse these for half the blocks
C square (with isolated motif if wanted)

Piecing

Sew and cut method can be used : make strips of
C + D and C + L. Complete blocks with the addition
of long D or L rectangle. Make equal numbers (or as
calculated) of each of the blocks.

BLOCK DESIGN 10

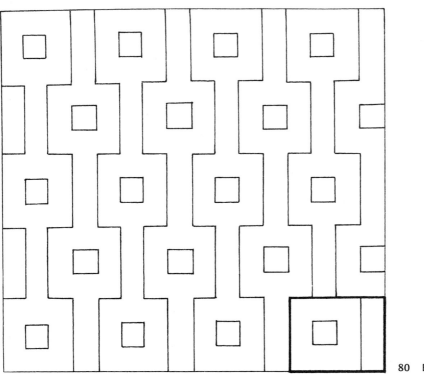

80 Block 10 pattern

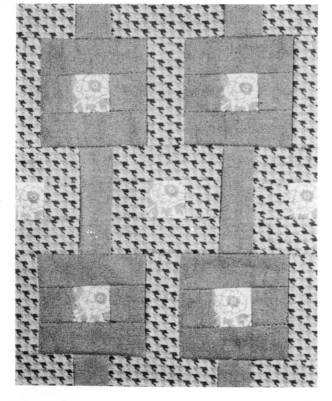

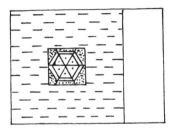

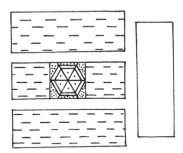

81   Rectangular 4 x 3 block, 6 pieces

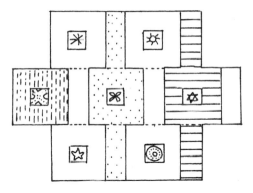

82 a   Assemble with shift

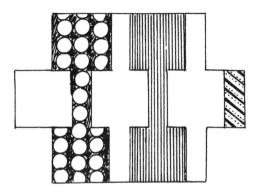

b   Pattern omitting small squares

Templates
3 x 1 rectangle, 1 x 1 square

Cutting (D block)
D two rectangles, two squares
L one rectangle
C one square

Piecing
Use sew and cut unless C isolates a motif, when it may not be possible. Make D and L blocks.

Assembly
Assemble in strips, with colour reversal and a shift in alternate rows (part blocks are needed). There are no points or seams to be matched.

Comments
For working out final size, remember that this is a rectangular block and not a square one.

Different colours could be used here for the vertical ring-and-link rows. Make a full colour plan.

A simpler version of this pattern can be made by omitting the central squares. Join 3 x 3 squares and 3 x 1 rectangles and assemble with colour change and half shift.

BLOCK DESIGN 11

83 Block 11 pattern

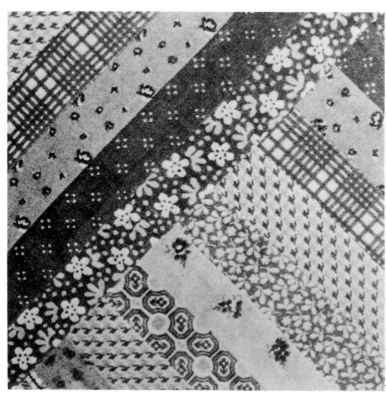

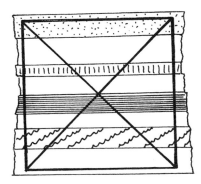

84 a   Cut triangles from joined strips

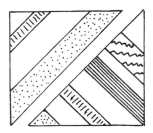

b   Block (any size) consists of 2 pieces

Templates

One for width of strips, or several if this varies, and right angled triangle with short side of desired block size (halve drawn block diagonally and add SA)

Cutting 1

Cut or tear strips of material of any width (same or different) and the length of the long side of the triangle template.

Piecing 1

Join enough strips to make a square.

Cutting 2

Cut square into four triangles from template.

Piecing 2

Join long sides of triangles in pairs so that stripes meet at right angles. Four triangles make two blocks.

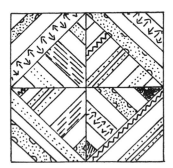

85   Assembly in fours

Assembly

Join blocks in fours, turning as shown. Assemble further in strips or larger blocks, matching seams.

Comments

This block is ideal for scrap use; a single block makes an effective cushion cover.

A straight repeat of blocks gives a diagonal pattern, which could be reflected. Plain material can be used in half of each block.

Note that diagram 83 shows a planned arrangement of even-width strips which calls for exact matching.

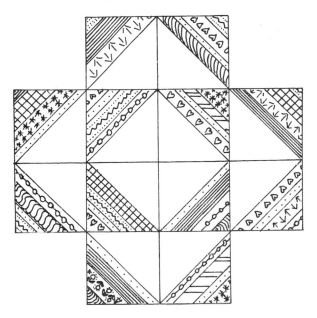

86   With plain half block, reflected

BLOCK DESIGN 12

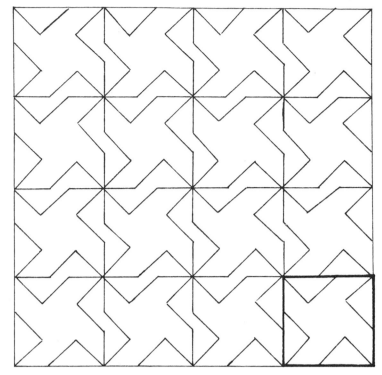

87   Block 12 pattern

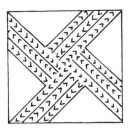

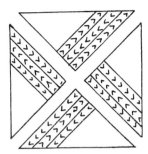

88   3 x 3 block, 8 pieces

89 a   Alternate blocks colour-changed

Templates
Triangle with long side 2, quadrilateral (UK trapezium, US trapezoid)

Cutting
D four quadrilaterals
L four triangles

Piecing
Join triangles to quadrilaterals, matching right angles for placement (triangle point protrudes). Four of the larger triangles formed make one block. Match centre seams when sewing together.

Sew and cut
Cut L strips the height of the triangle template.
D strips are the height of the quadrilateral. To cut quarter block triangles from strips, make a template from a diagonal quarter of the block, plus SA. Watch the positioning of the templates on the strip so that D and L are correct. See page 34.

Assembly
Match corners and assemble in strips or blocks.

Comments
This is a well-known traditional block in America, where versions of it are known as *Whirlwind* and *Windmill*. The D could easily be scrap colours.

Alternate coloured blocks give interlocked motifs, with great care needing in matching. Reflected blocks give an allover diamond pattern. Note that proportions can be changed (as in many other blocks) by using a different unit size of block.

b   Reflected pattern

BLOCK DESIGN 13

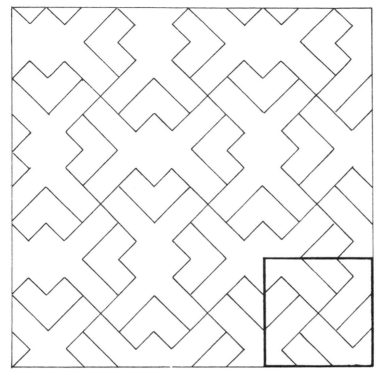

90 Block 13 pattern

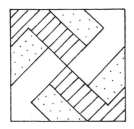

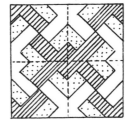

92 Assembly in fours

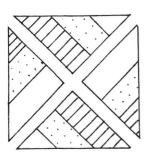

91 3 x 3 block, 12 pieces

Templates
Triangle with long side 1, quadrilaterals (UK trapezium, US trapezoid) of two sizes

Cutting
D two long quadrilaterals, two triangles
L two long quadrilaterals, two triangles
C four short quadrilaterals

Piecing
Make up quarter block triangles, observing correct colouring (two have long D, two have long L). Assemble four quarters to make the block, matching the centre. Flip templates over for reflected blocks.

Sew and cut
Cut or tear strips of D, L and C join, and cut large triangles from quarter block template. Watch positioning of template for triangles needed.

Assembly
Join blocks, reflected, in fours, and continue assembly in blocks or strips.

Comments
Each long cross in this arrangement extends over four blocks, so any version using scraps would need very careful planning indeed with constant reference to a drawn out and coloured plan.

93　Block 14 pattern

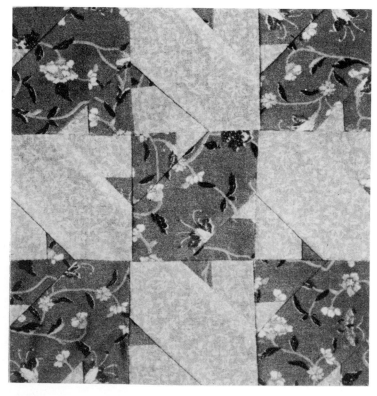

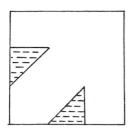

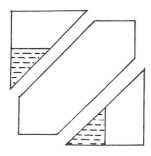

94   3 x 3 block, 5 pieces

Templates
Long hexagon, 1 x 1 triangle, quadrilateral (UK trapezium, US trapezoid)

Cutting (L block)
D two triangles
L one hexagon, two quad-
rilaterals

Piecing
Join triangles to short parallel side of quadrilaterals; then join two of these on either long side of the hexagon to form the blunt arrow figure. Make D and L blocks.

Sew and cut
Cut or tear D and L strips, measuring height from templates. Make a 2 x 2 triangle template to cut triangles from strips. Be sure you cut the right triangles with regard to shapes and colouring.

Assembly
Join alternate coloured blocks in blocks of four, turning so that the arrows follow round in a clock-

wise direction. Match corners, and try to match the side seams of blocks too, but the corners matter more. Assemble further in blocks or strips.

Comments
Scraps can be used for one of the tones, but each winged arrow extends over three blocks, so care will be needed.

Study of the pattern will show that there is a square at the junction of four blocks which can be picked up and used as a block. It has the same lines as Block 12, but with a colour change in two triangles.

Note that the photograph shows altered proportions of the block.

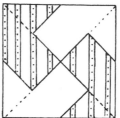

96   Further block from pattern

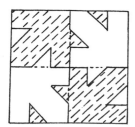

95   Assembly in fours

BLOCK DESIGN 15

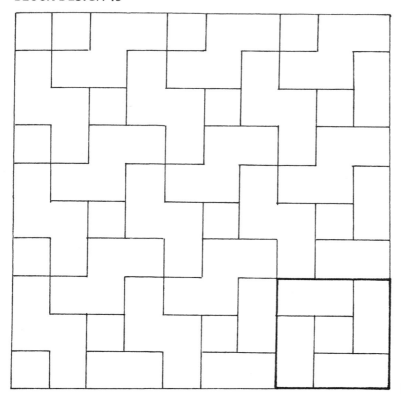

97 Block 15 pattern

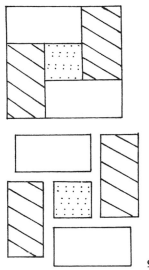

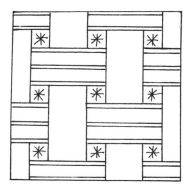

99 a   Reflected pattern

98   3 x 3 block, 5 pieces

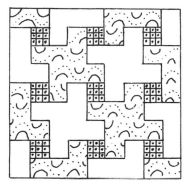

b   Pattern with turning

Templates
2 x 1 rectangle, 1 x 1 square

Cutting
D two rectangles
L two rectangles
C one square

Piecing
Use half open seam technique : join half of the one
side of the square to a rectangle, and continue adding
rectangles to the long straight sides until all four have
been joined on. Complete first seam, starting from
the middle. See page 34.

Assembly
Assemble in blocks or strips, matching corners.

Comments
Note that this is a half open seam version of the
pattern from Block 3. Four colours can be used
for the weave effect instead of two, but be careful
to set all the blocks the same way.

Reflection gives a fat weave; turning alternate blocks
reverses D and L and yields interlocking D and L
figures.

BLOCK DESIGN 16

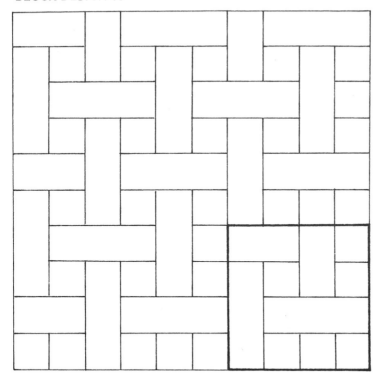

100   Block 16 pattern

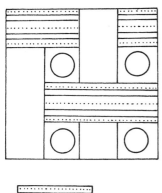

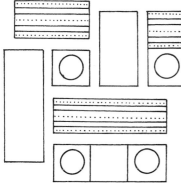

101 4 x 4 block, 10 pieces

Comments
For the open weave effect, colouring must remain constant, so this is not a suitable pattern for the use of scraps of random colours. This is a half open seam version, with altered proportions, of the pattern from Block 9.

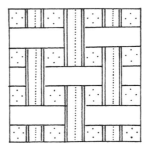

102 Quarter blocks omitted

Templates
3 x 1 rectangle, 2 x 1 rectangle, 1 x 1 square

Cutting
D one rectangle of each size, one square
L one rectangle of each size, one square
C four squares

Piecing
Using sew and cut if you want, join three pieces to make 2 x 2 section at top right, then four pieces to make 3 x 2 section at bottom right. You now have five pieces, including the top left C square. This square is the pivot around which you join the other four pieces, using a hlaf open seam. Half seam the square to the L part of the 2 x 2 square, and continue round in a clockwise direction, always adding to a straight edge. Finish the block by completing the first half seam from the centre outwards to the edge of the block.

Assembly
Assemble in blocks or strips, matching corners and seams very carefully as exact joins are needed for the effect of the pattern. Add quarter strips (or omit quarter blocks) to let the C squares sit symmetrically.

BLOCK DESIGN 17

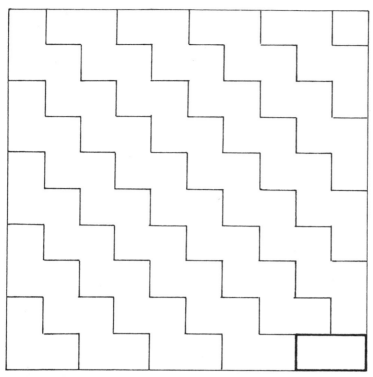

103 Block 17 pattern

Block Design 29

Block Design 27

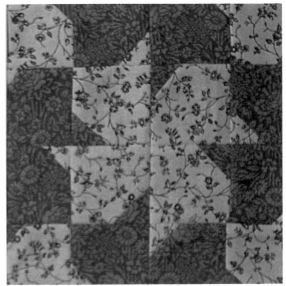

Three cushions: (left) all-over half-seam pattern, (centre) Block Design
13, (right) Block Design 40

Block Design 18

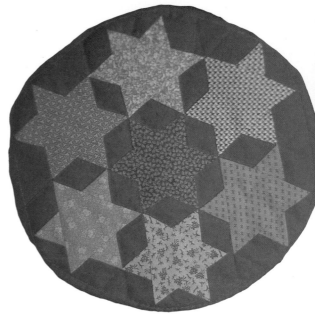

Stool cover: Block Design 24

Cot quilt: Block Design 30, with interposed plain blocks

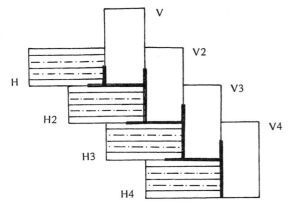

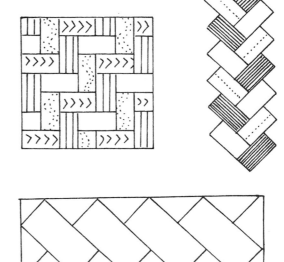

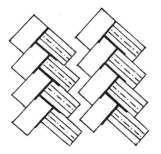

104 a Individual strip

b Joining strips

105 Weave and plait effect; plait border

Templates
2 x 1 rectangle, 1 x 1 square to fill in at edges.

Cutting
Equal numbers of D and L rectangles, plus squares as necessary.

Piecing
Using the half open seam technique, make strips of rectangles as follows : half seam the top horizontal rectangle (H) to the top vertical rectangle (V); add H2, leaving a part seam open at the left; add V2, again leaving an open part seam. Continue working like this in a general V-shape.

Assembly
Work with two strips in a Λ-shape with points facing up. All seams now complete previous half seams. Subsequent strips are joined on in the same way.
1 x 1 squares (half rectangles) must be added to get straight edges. Seams terminating at the edge of the work can be sewn their entire length at the start.

Comments
Different colourings can be tried to give weave and plait effects. These will be lost with scrap colouring unless close attention is paid to choice of tones.

A plait border can be pieced without half seams by first joining 1 x 1 triangles to the ends of rectangles.

BLOCK DESIGN 18

106   Block 18 pattern

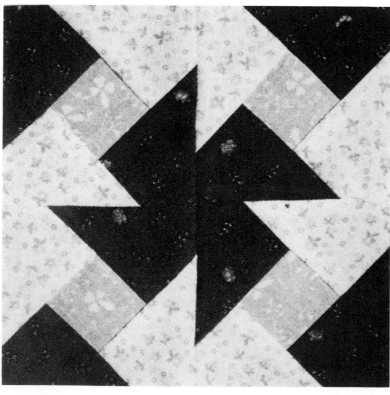

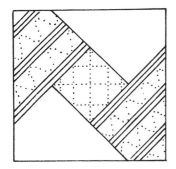

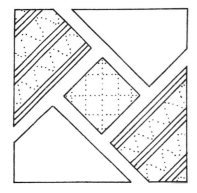

107   4 x 4 block, 5 pieces

pattern as Block 7, set diagonally (match points on sides carefully).

The block can be modified and worked in two colours only to give a lattice pattern.

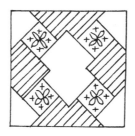

108 a Reflected pattern

 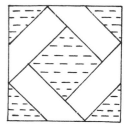

b Lattice pattern and modified block

Templates
Square one *diagonal* unit on each side, quadrilateral with opposite right angles

Cutting
D two quadrilaterals
L two quadrilaterals
C one square

Piecing
Use half open seam technique around the C square as in Block 15, the only difference being that the seams here are not at right angles to block sides.

Assembly
Assemble in blocks or strips, with all blocks set straight. This is a tolerant and forgiving block where meeting corners are all of one colour, and there is no matching of block sides either.

Comments
Overall use of scraps for one tone might be effective, but remember that one figure extends over four blocks, and make a detailed plan accordingly. Make sure that the C tone is different from both of the others, or else only one set of figures will show, as motifs powdered on a background.

Four blocks can be reflected to give almost the same

BLOCK DESIGN 19

109 Block 19 pattern

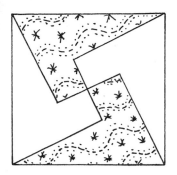

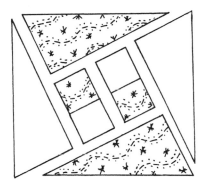

110   2 x 2 block, 8 pieces

Templates
Square, long right angled triangle (see *Comments* below)

Cutting
D two squares, two triangles
L two squares, two traingles

Piecing
Make the central square first, using sew and cut if you want; match corners carefully, Then add on the triangles, right angles to the centre, leaving the first seam half open. In this version of the block you work round the centre anti-clockwise. Finish the block by completing the first half seam.

Assembly
Assemble blocks in fours, using two blocks as above and two reflected blocks. The narrow angles at block corners need careful matching. Complete assembly in strips or larger blocks.

Comments
This block is known as *Arabic Lattice* in America, and is regarded as a difficult block to piece. Using a half open seam, however, it is not difficult to sew by machine.

To draw the block, join each corner to the centre point of the opposite side, and quarter the square in the middle by measuring (its lines do not lie on the grid lines, but the centre of the cross should fall on the centre point of the block).

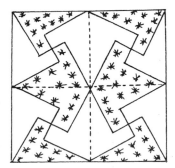

111   Assembly in fours

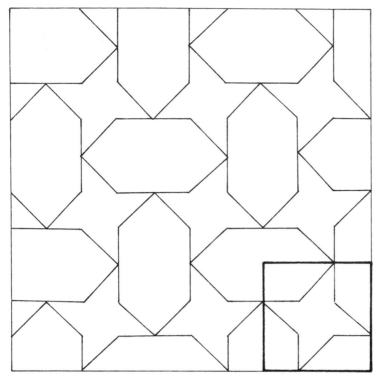

112   Block 20 pattern

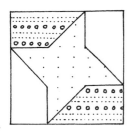

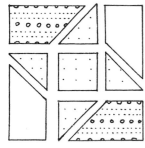

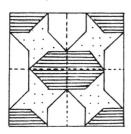
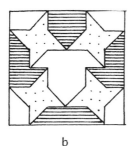

113 3 x 3 block, 9 pieces

Templates
Quadrilateral (UK trapezium, US trapezoid), 1 x 1 square, 1 x 1 triangle

Cutting
D two quadrilaterals
L two quadrilaterals
C one square, four triangles

Piecing
Join two D and two L quadrilaterals to C triangles, giving four rectangles, which are joined around the C square starting with a half open seam. Complete the block by closing the rest of the first seam. Reflected blocks are worked in an anti-clockwise direction, the pieces being cut from reversed templates.

Assembly
Join into blocks of four (two reflected blocks), matching triangle points on block sides. Corners are less important.

a   b

114 a Assembly in fours
   b Rearrangement of four blocks to give arks

Comments
This star figures in more than one traditional block. It produces several interesting patterns.

A rearrangement of the four-block gives a pattern of stars and arcs. Using only the basic block without the reflected version, turn alternate blocks to reverse D and L for a star and windmill pattern. Piecing the block itself differently, with rectangles turned round, yields a new block with further possibilities.

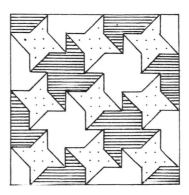

115 a Stars and windmills

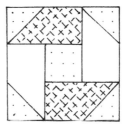

   b Further block with rectangles reversed

BLOCK DESIGN 21

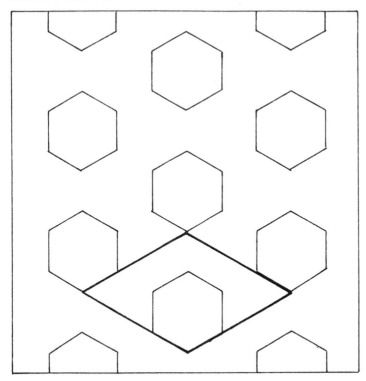

116   Block 21 pattern

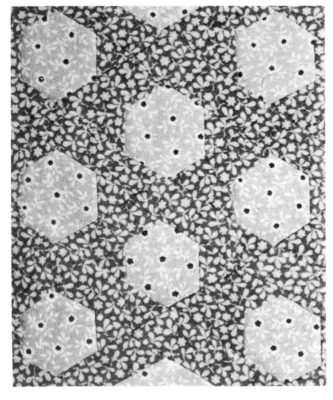

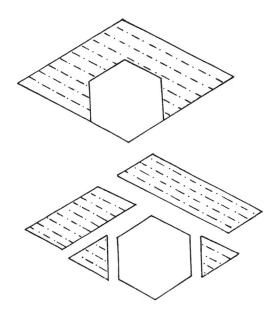

Templates
1 hexagon, 1 triangle, 2 x 1 and 3 x 1 parallelograms

Cutting
D two triangles, one of each parallelogram
L one hexagon

Piecing
Join triangles to opposite sides of the hexagon, then add short and long parallelograms to complete the diamond block.

Assembly
Assemble in vertical or diagonal strips. See page 32 for diamond assembly to form a rectangle. All seam lines ought to be matched, but the pattern will not be spoilt if corners are not exact.

Comments
There is no difficulty about using scrap colouring for the hexagons. The background should remain the same.

Turning alternate blocks, or rows, gives paired hexagons in diagonal sequence; background colours could change every two rows for vertical stripes.

Note that diamonds can easily be made by cutting L hexagon and triangles in one, making a block of only three pieces. These can be arranged with hexagons or used on their own.

117   Isometric 3 x 3, 5 pieces

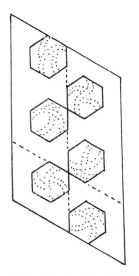

118   Turning for paired hexagons

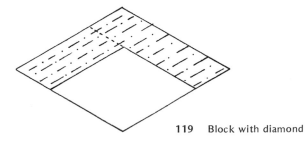

119   Block with diamond

BLOCK DESIGN 22

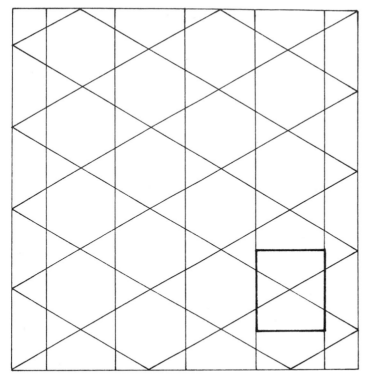

120   Block 22 pattern

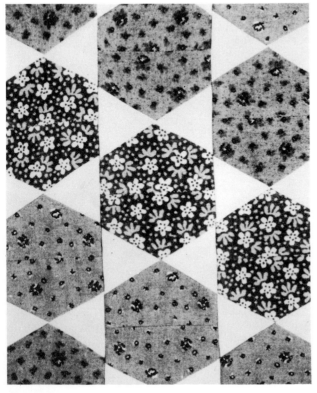

82

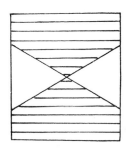 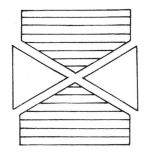

121   Rectangular block on isometric paper, 4 pieces

Templates
Pentagon (half hexagon), 1 triangle

Cutting
D two pentagons
L two triangles

Piecing
Join triangles to pentagons and sew these halves together, matching the triangle points, and placing them carefully for sewing as shown.

Assembly
Assemble in vertical strips with a half block drop so that triangle points meet. Minor adjustments can be made at this stage by taking in or letting out the block seams which fall at mid-hexagon (some hexagon sides may be off-true in size if you adjust like this, but it won't spoil the overall effect, which mismatched triangle points certainly will). Trim off protruding half blocks — this is easier than making part blocks.

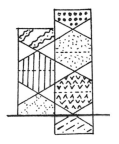

122   Assemble with half drop; trim edges

Comments
Note that each finished hexagon is formed from two parts of different blocks. Scrap colouring of hexagons is possible with reference to a full plan. Random colouring is easier to handle if you use diamond blocks, cutting each hexagon in one and

adding triangles, but this allows of no adjustment at the assembly stage. You can make a border this way.

For calculation of final size, remember that this a a rectangular block.

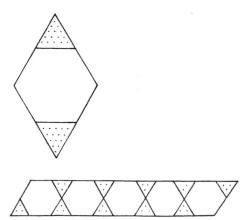

123   2 x 2 diamond block; border

BLOCK DESIGN 23

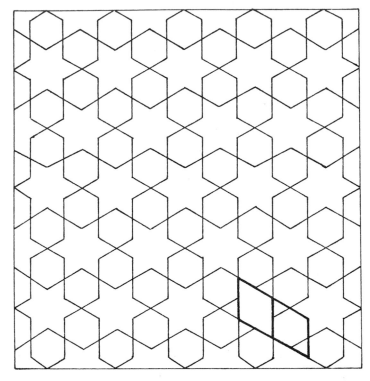

124   Block 23 pattern

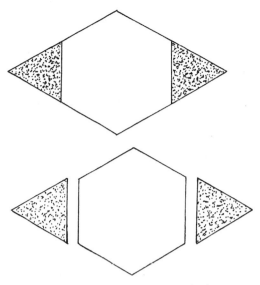

one block drop or shift so that stars are surrounded by rings of hexagons. See *Diamond Assembly*, page 32.

Comments
Closely related to Block 22, this could also be sewn using rectangular blocks in sequence.

Scraps could be used for one of the tones, or even throughout if they can be chosen to be unambiguously D or L.

125   Isometric 2 x 2 block, 3 pieces (+1)

Templates
1 hexagon, 1 triangle, 2 diamond

Cutting
D two triangles, full block diamond
L one hexagon

Piecing
Join triangles to opposite sides of hexagon to make diamond block.

Assembly
Assemble in vertical or diagonal strips, in the sequence 2 pieced diamonds, 1 plain diamond, matching meeting triangle points. Join strips with

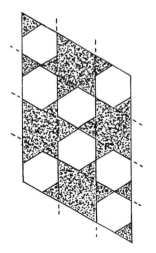

126   Sequence for assembly

BLOCK DESIGN 24

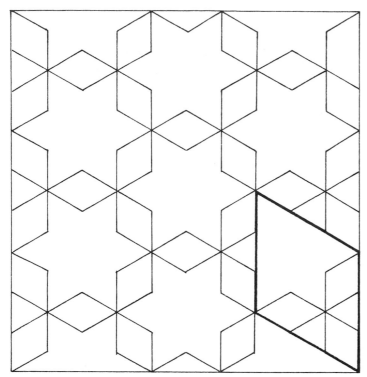

127   Block 24 pattern

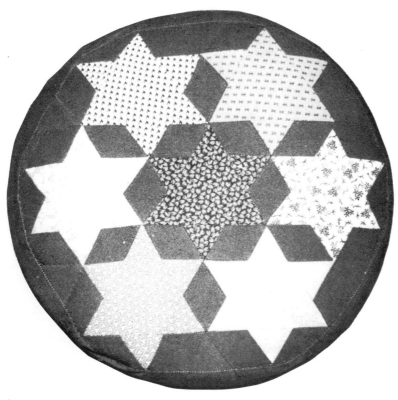

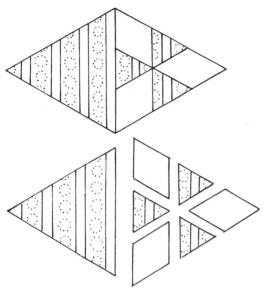

Assembly
Assemble in vertical or diagonal strips, matching corners. See *Diamond Assembly,* page 32.

Comments
Any random colouring of stars would need to be closely planned. The piece shown is filled in with background colour at the edges.

The three-legged figures can be emphasised by using different colours for each set of diamonds.

128   Isometric 3 x 3 block, 7 pieces

Templates
3 triangle, 1 triangle, 1 diamond

Cutting
D one large triangle, three small triangles
L three diamonds

Piecing
Join two L diamonds to a small D triangle, then two D triangles to the third L diamond. Sew these together, matching points, and join to large D triangle to form the diamond block.

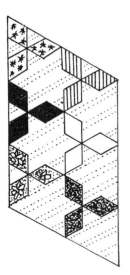

129   Sets of diamonds emphasised

BLOCK DESIGN 25

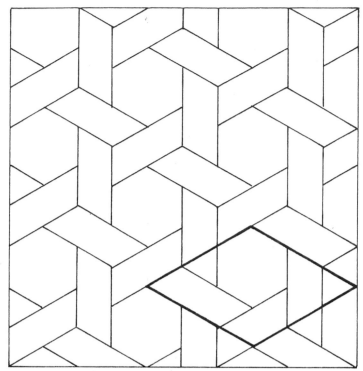

130   Block 25 pattern

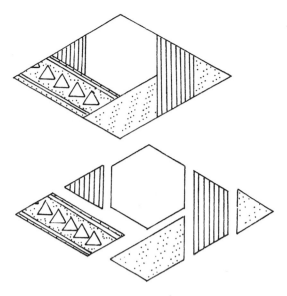

blocks — exact matching is vital, (See *Diamond Assembly*, page 32).

Comments
This is an effective pattern which must be assembled with precision. All seams must lie exactly right for the three-way weave to be clear and attractive.

Scraps could be used for the hexagons, but not for the weave pieces. Patterned weave pieces would show the seam joins less, but might make it more difficult to read the overall pattern.

131   Isometric 3 x 3 block, 6 pieces

Templates
1 hexagon, 1 triangle, 2 parrallelogram, quadrilateral (UK trapezium, US trapezoid)

Cutting
D one triangle, one quadrilateral
L one hexagon
C1 one parallelogram
C2 one triangle, one quadrilateral

Piecing
Start by joining D triangle to one side of the hexagon, and continue joining on the other pieces from left to right. Refer back often to a drawn out block as it's easy to get confused.

Assembly
Assemble in vertical or diagonal strips; match corners and points where like coloured pieces join on sides of

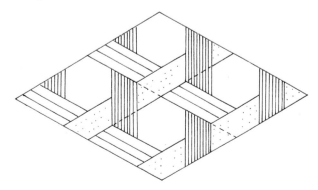

132   Exact matching in assembly

89

BLOCK DESIGN 26

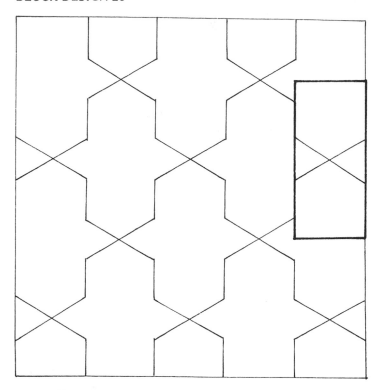

133   Block 26 pattern

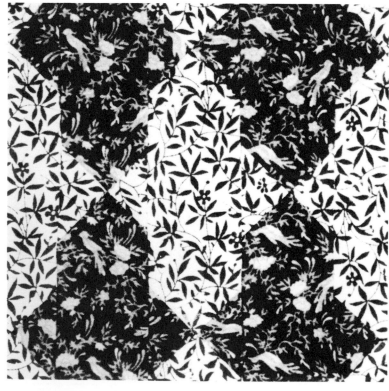

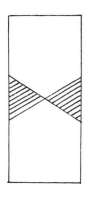
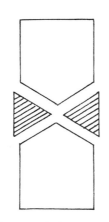

minor variations of block-centring do not matter. Trim edges straight, or use an easy part block.

Comments
With care an element of random colouring can be introduced, but tone alternation must be retained for easy reading of the pattern.

For calculation of final size, note that this is a rectangular block. Proportions can easily be varied with this block — you can make long thin brackets or short fat ones.

Compare Block 22, of which this is an easy variation.

134   Rectangular block on isometric paper, 4 pieces

Templates
Pentagon, 1 triangle

Cutting (L block)
D two triangles
L two pentagons

Piecing
Make block in two halves by joining a triangle to a pentagon and joining these, matching triangle points. Make D and L blocks.

Assembly
Assemble in vertical strips of D and L blocks, with a half drop between strips so that the horizontal block seams come in the middle of adjacent blocks' triangles. No close matching is needed, and provided triangle points were matched at the block stage,

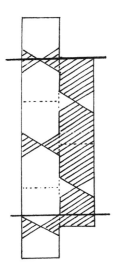

135   Assemble with half drop; the top shows the trimmed edge, the bottom shows the easy part block

BLOCK DESIGN 27

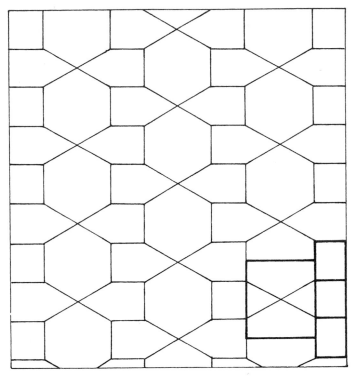

136   Block 27 pattern

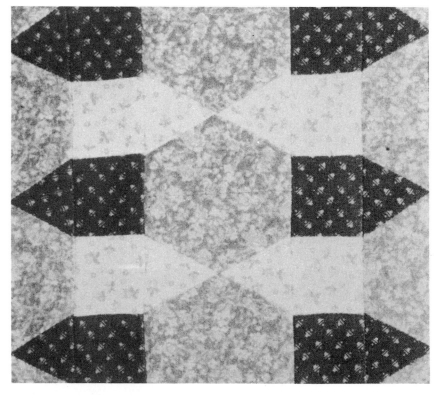

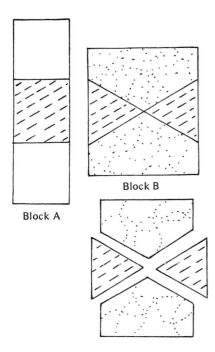

Block B

Block A

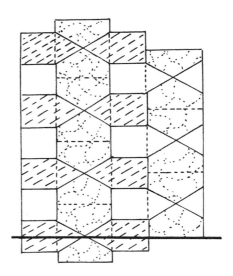

138 Assembly sequence; trim straight

137 Rectangular blocks on isometric paper; Block A : 4 pieces; Block B : 1 piece

Templates
Pentagon (half hexagon), 1 triangle, rectangle

Cutting (D block)
Block A D two triangles
       C two pentagons
Block B D and L rectangles

Piecing
Join triangles to pentagons to make two halves, then join these, matching triangle points. Made D and L blocks.

Assembly
Make strips of D and L rectangles. These strips (B) alternate with vertically joined Block A strips, in the sequence B, Block A dark, B, Block A light etc. Match rectangles and triangles of like colouring.

Comments
Only the hexagons could conveniently be randomly coloured in this pattern, and even then their tones should be kept close and in contrast to the tones of the pentagons.

A row of hexagons flanked by two rows of rectangles makes a good border.

This is a more difficult version of the pattern from Block 26, with the motifs set horizontally and broken up.

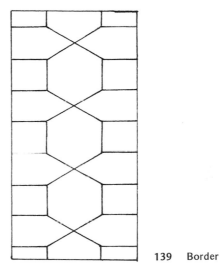

139 Border

BLOCK DESIGN 28

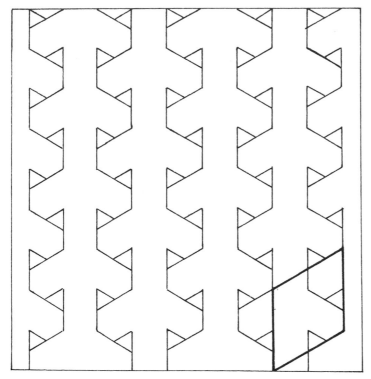

140 Block 28 pattern

94

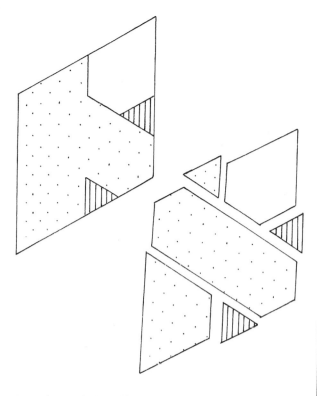

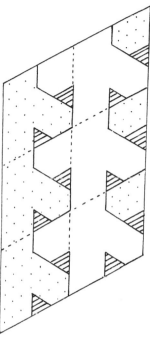

141   Isometric 4 x 4 block, 6 pieces

142   Assembly

Templates
Long hexagon, 1 triangle, pentagon, quadrilateral (UK trapezium, US trapezoid)

A border could be made from a strip of blocks with an added strip of the pentagon colour.

Cutting (D block)
D one hexagon, one triangle,
one quadrilateral
L one pentagon
C two triangles

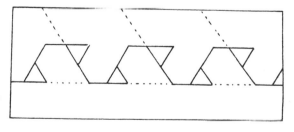

143   Border with added strip

Piecing
Join two triangles to the pentagon, and one triangle to the quadrilateral. Join these large triangles to the long sides of the hexagon, watching positioning so that the C triangles face across the hexagon. Make D and L blocks.

Assembly
Assemble in vertical strips of D and L blocks, matching centre sides of blocks to form the continuing lines of the pattern. Join the vertical strips, matching as closely as possible. Minor mismatching will not throw the pattern off, but through-going lines ought to be straight for best effect. (*See Diamond Assembly*, page 32.)

BLOCK DESIGN 29

144   Block 29 pattern

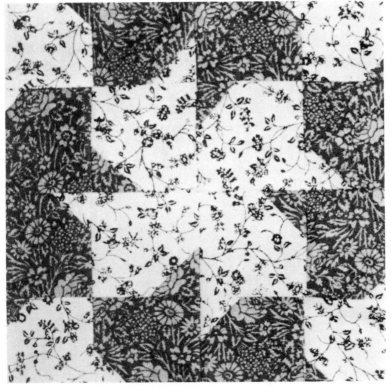

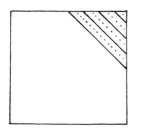 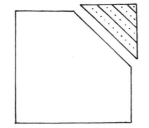

145   2 x 2 block, 2 pieces

Templates
Pentagon, 1 x 1 triangle

Cutting (L block)
D one triangle
L one pentagon

Piecing
Join triangle to pentagon side opposite right angle to make block. Make D and L blocks.

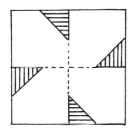

146   Assembly in fours

Assembly
Assemble sets of four D and L blocks with successive clockwise blocks turned 90° Join four-blocks in bigger blocks or strips, alternating colours and matching centre sides of blocks exactly.

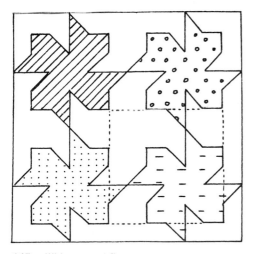

147   Wider spaced flowers

Comments
Either D or L 'flowers' could be made in random colours, but one flower is made up of pieces in four 2 x 2 blocks as well as the central four-block, so exact adherence to a plan is necessary at both piecing and assembly stages.

An arrangement of eight 2 x 2 blocks and one solid one gives wider spaced flowers.

There are several other interesting arrangements of this block (See pages 24-5.)

BLOCK DESIGN 30

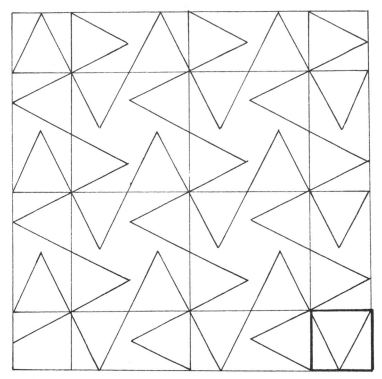

148 Block 30 pattern

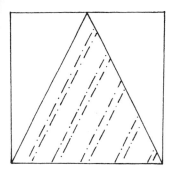

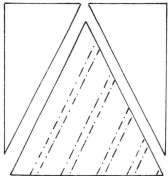

149   2 x 2 block, 3 pieces

Templates
Triangle, long right angled triangle

Cutting
D one triangle
L two long triangles

Piecing
Join one L triangle on each side of the D triangle, placing carefully for sewing. Note that the tops of the D triangles do not reach the edge of the block.

Assembly
Join blocks in fours, turning successive blocks 90°. Matching of centres is difficult because of the narrow angles where eight pieces meet. For an allover cross or vane pattern, join these four-blocks, matching triangle points at centre sides of blocks. For the

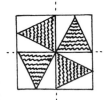

150   Assembly of vanes and diamonds

alternating diamond pattern of the photograph, join four blocks as shown, and alternate in assembly.

Comments
The care needed in assembling these blocks is more than compensated by their suitability for scrap use and the variety of possible arrangements.

For easier matching, alternate plain blocks (See diagram 229 on page 133.) Create an allover star and octagon pattern by assembling four pieced and five plain blocks in nines. Powder random colours of stars closely on a ground (following a colour plan) by assembling 2 x 2 blocks in strips. Use a row of four-blocks as a border, with crosses and diamonds in regular sequence.

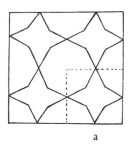

a   b

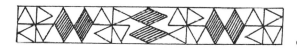

c

151 a   Four pieced and five plain blocks
b   Stars on background
c   Cross and diamond border

99

BLOCK DESIGN 31

152   Block 31 pattern

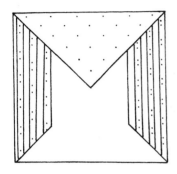

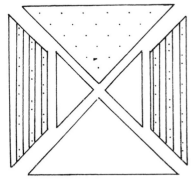

153   4 x 4 block, 6 pieces

Templates
Quarter block triangle, small triangle, quadrilateral
(UK trapezium, US trapezoid)

Cutting (L block)
D two quadrilaterals
L one large triangle,
two small triangles
C one large triangle

Piecing
Join L triangles to quadrilaterals; join resulting
triangles to L and C triangles, and complete block by
a diagonal seam joining the two halves (match centre
seams). Also make blocks with L and C reversed.

Assembly
Join blocks in horizontal strips of L and C blocks,
matching D pieces to form long hexagons. Join

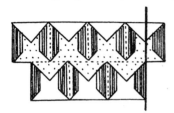

154   Assemble with half shift; trim sides

alternate L and C strips with half shift so that long
hexagons come below triangles. Trim sides straight to
avoid making half blocks.

Comments
The zigzag horizontals can be of random or
alternating colours. Cut and assemble one row at a
time for random colouring, remembering that the C
tone in one row becomes L in the next.

One horizontal row can be used as a border, perhaps
with added L and C strips.

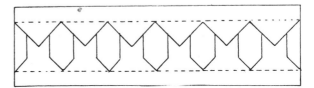

155   Border with added strips

BLOCK DESIGN 32

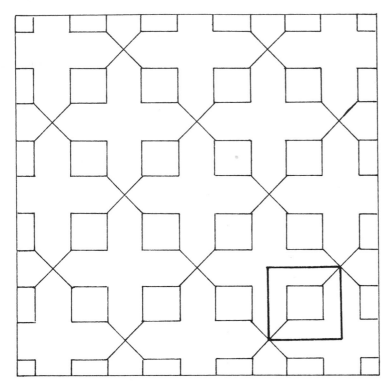

156   Block 32 pattern

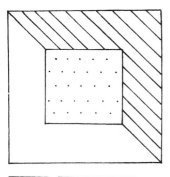

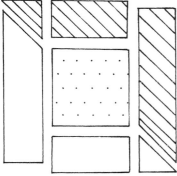

157 4 x 4 block, 7 pieces

Templates
2 x 2 square, 2 x 1 rectangle, 1 x 1 triangle, quadrilateral (UK trapezium, US trapezoid)

Cutting
D one rectangle, one triangle, one quadrilateral
L one rectangle, one triangle, one quadrilateral
C one square

Piecing
Join D and L rectangles to C square, then join triangles to opposite colour quadrilaterals. The rectangles formed go on either side of the central rectangle to make the diagonally halved 'frame'.

Assembly
Assemble blocks in fours to form a pointed cross

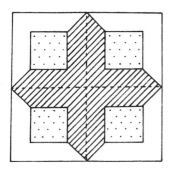

158 Assembly in fours

framed by the other tone. To assemble four-blocks, work in strips, matching where points meet (corners have like colours).

Comments
Random colouring can be used for one tone, but keep the other constant for best effect.

With altered proportions (to 3 x 3 block) and only two colours, a straight repeat produces the star and pointed cross pattern often seen in Islamic decoration.

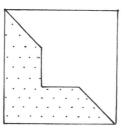

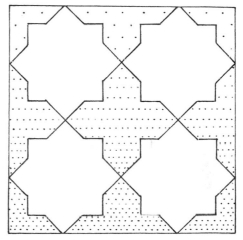

159 3 x 3 block and pattern

BLOCK DESIGN 33

160 Block 33 pattern

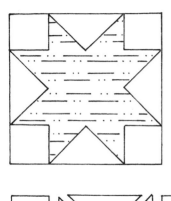

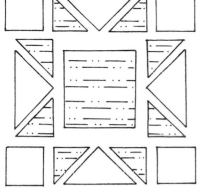

of the comparatively large number of pieces in the block, it is not very difficult, and can be made quite large without being overpowering.

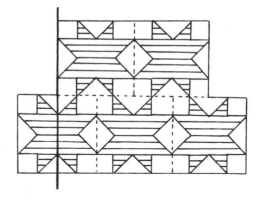

162   Assemble with half shift; trim sides

161   4 x 4 block, 17 pieces

Templates
2 x 2 square, 1 x 1 square, 1 x 1 triangle, 2 x 2 triangle measured diagonally

Cutting
D one large square, eight small triangles
L four small squares, four large triangles

Piecing
Join two D triangles to each L triangle, forming rectangles. To two of these rectangles join L squares (NB outer D triangle points do not reach edge of block). Join other two rectangles to opposite sides of D square. Complete block by adding long rectangles at edges.

Assembly
Assemble blocks in horizontal strips, matching star points, and forming squares between stars. Join strips with half shift, matching star points to form pentagons. Shifted rows need half blocks at ends.

Comments
This star occurs in several traditional patterns. It is included because of its suitability for scraps and for the added interest created by the half shift. In spite

BLOCK DESIGN 34

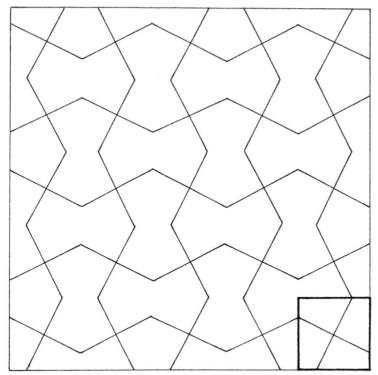

163   Block 34 pattern

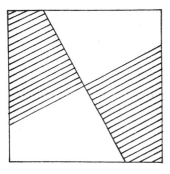

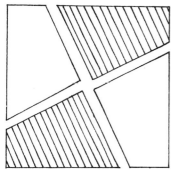

164   4 x 4 block, 4 pieces

Template
Irregular quadrilateral with two right angles

Cutting
D two pieces
L two pieces

Piecing
Join opposite colour pieces in pairs, referring often to a drawn out block, as the right angles can confuse you. Join two halves to complete the block, matching centre seams. Make an equal number of reflected blocks (flip template over to mark and cut).

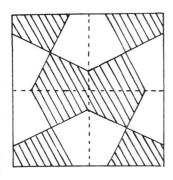

165   Assembly in fours

Assembly
Either assemble in strips of alternating blocks, starting each strip with a different block, or assemble in fours and repeat this four-block straight. However you assemble you must match points on all four block sides, but corners join like colours, so need be exactly matched only by perfectionists.

Comments
This is a simple but baffling pattern (try to draw it out without looking back at it). Random colouring would need a lot of planning at every stage.

A straight repeat of the block with alternate D and L plain blocks produces an interlock of a rather squat twelve-sided figure.

Combinations of reflection and colour change give further variations of interlocked figures, including the interesting one shown.

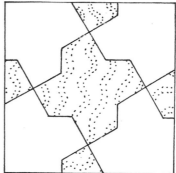

166   Further patterns

BLOCK DESIGN 35

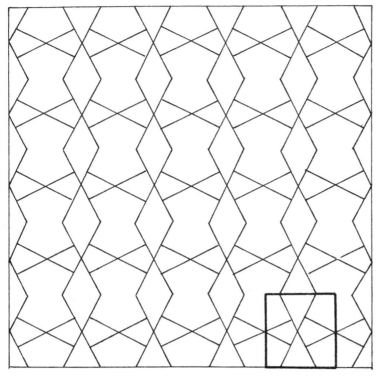

167   Block 35 pattern

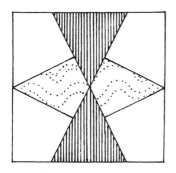

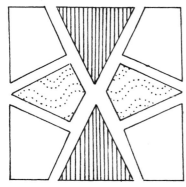

168   4 x 4 block, 8 pieces

Templates
Triangle, regular kite shape, quadrilateral (see below for alternative isometric version)

Cutting
D two triangles
L four quadrilaterals
C two regular kites

Piecing
Join two L shapes to long sides of C kites. Add D triangles to make half blocks, and join halves, matching points of D triangles.

Assembly
Join blocks in strips, matching D triangle bases to form diamonds. Join strips matching points of C pieces. Matching of corners is secondary.

Comments
For scrap use, lines of diamonds could be of different colours, either all different, or with each line matching. Differently coloured horizontal 'diamonds' (C) would be even easier to handle.

A vertical row of blocks would make a good border, either in three tones or only two.

Isometric version
Drawn on isometric paper, the block needs only two

templates, the triangle and the kite. Assemble the block shown into horizontal strips, and turn alternate strips upside down before joining. this gives a pattern of divided hexagons separated by rows of diamonds. Note that the isometric block is rectangular, not square.

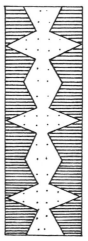

169   Two-colour border

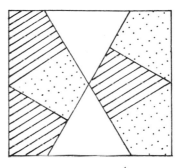

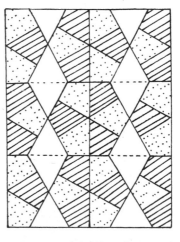

170   Rectangular block (isometric) and pattern

109

BLOCK DESIGN 36

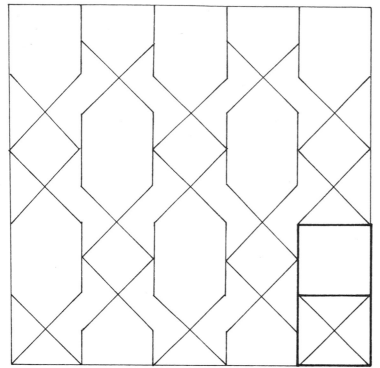

171 Block 36 pattern

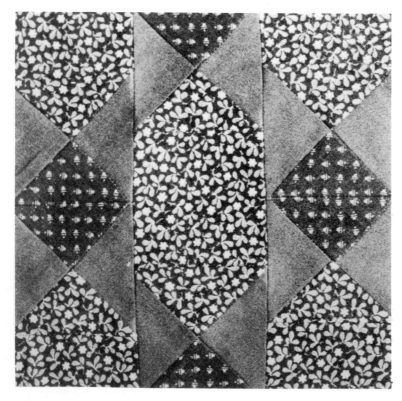

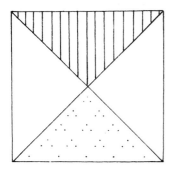

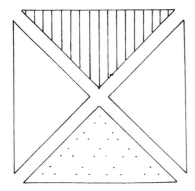

172   2 x 2 block, 4 pieces (+1)

Templates
Triangle, whole block square

Cutting
D one triangle (and whole blocks)
L two triangles
C one triangle

Piecing
Join D and L triangle, L and C triangle. Matching the centre, complete block with diagonal seam joining two halves.

Assembly
Join in vertical strips of one D block, two pieced blocks, matching contrast triangles to form squares. Join strips with half drop so that C squares come at the mid point of long D hexagons. Use half a plain block at top and bottom of half the number of strips.

Comments
Scrap colouring is possible for long hexagons or C squares; or else hexagons and squares can be one colour, with the 'feet' motifs picked out in groups.

If you add a plain C block and use the sequence C, pieced, D, pieced, C etc, the result is a squared version of Block 22. This can be sewn with less piecing using another block.

For a border, use a vertical strip of the original sequence, or a pair of strips.

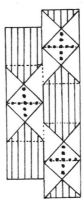

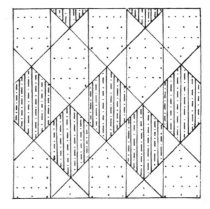

173   Assemble with half drop

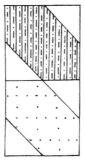

174   Pattern with C block; alternative block

BLOCK DESIGN 37

175   Block 37 pattern

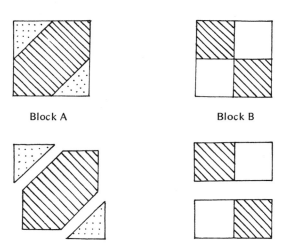

Block A   Block B

176   2 x 2 blocks; Block A : 3 pieces, Block B : 4 pieces

This pattern is of course a development of Block 1, with lopped off C corners to the plain blocks. This is a straightforward way of elaborating many simple patterns.

Templates
Long hexagon, 1 x 1 triangle, 1 x 1 square

Cutting (D block)
Block A   D one hexagon
           C two triangles
Block B   D two squares
           L two squares

Piecing
Make equal numbers of Block A in D and L by joining C triangles to D and L hexagons. Use sew and cut method for Block B if you want, cutting with a 2 x 1 template.

Assembly
Assemble four-blocks from a D and a L Block A and two quartered blocks. Note placing for joining : the quartered blocks always run the same way, and should be matched to the C triangles. Assemble four-blocks in strips or larger blocks.

Comments
Random colouring would be possible but not easy for either D or L — a full plan would be needed.

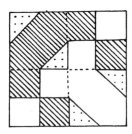

177   Assembly in fours

BLOCK DESIGN 38

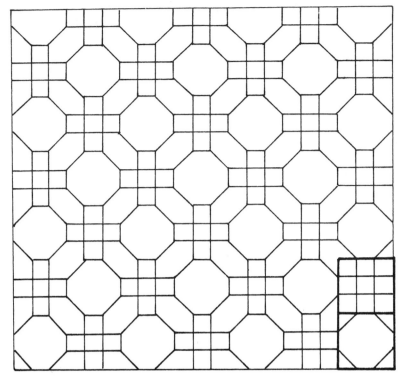

178   Block 38 pattern

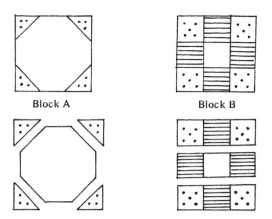

Block A   Block B

centre square of Block B can be D, making a cross (use a 3 x 1 template for this).

A 2 x 2 version of the block produces large over-lapping octagons formed by four hexagons and a square.

179   3 x 3 blocks; Block A : 5 pieces, Block B : 9 pieces

Templates
Octagon, 1 x 1 triangle, 1 x 1 square

Cutting
Block A   L one octagon
          C four triangles
Block B   D four squares
          L one square
          C four squares

Piecing
Join C triangles to correct four sides of L octagon. Use sew and cut (with 3 x 1 template) for Block B, matching seams exactly when joining the strips.

Assembly
Join A and B alternately in strips or blocks, always matching the C triangles to the C squares of Block B to form long diagonal hexagons in C. Matching of corners is secondary.

Comments
The C tone should stay the same throughout, but scrap colouring is possible for either L or D. The

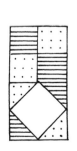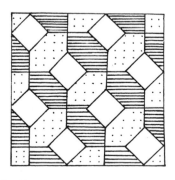

180   2 x 2 blocks and pattern

115

181 Block 39 pattern

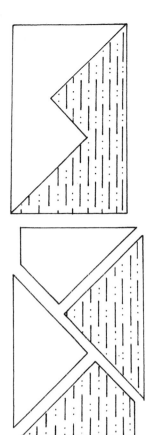

Choose firm materials for this block, as block seams are often joining pieces cut on the cross; if these pieces stretch during assembly, the work will never lie flat.

It is possible to make this pattern without using diagonals at all. It involves a complicated sequence of five 3 x 3 blocks with colour changes and a shift, and is better avoided, specially with the above easy repeat available. Always look hard at a pattern to see that you have chosen the simplest block.

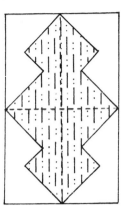

183   Assembly in fours

182   Rectangular 5 x 3 block, 4 pieces

Templates
Triangle, quadrilateral

Cutting
D one triangle, one quadrilateral
L one triangle, one quadrilateral

Piecing
Join L triangle and D quadrilateral with right angles together; join another pair of opposite colours, and complete the block with a diagonal seam. Reverse templates for quadrilateral pieces in reflected blocks.

Assembly
Join four blocks in reflection to form an entire motif surrounded by the other tone. Match points at outer edges of block joins (these points do not reach block edges, only to SA). Assemble further in strips or larger blocks, whichever is easier for the matching required.

Comments
One tone can easily be varied in colour here, perhaps to form whole lines of motifs in different colours.

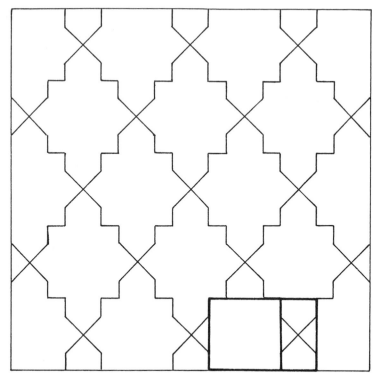

184   Block 40 pattern

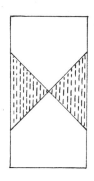
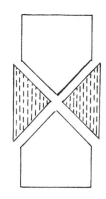

185 Rectangular 2 x 4 block, 4 pieces (+1)

Templates
Pentagon, triangle, whole (4 x 4) block square

Cutting
D two triangles
L two pentagons   make L block
(and D and L whole blocks)

Piecing
Join D triangles to L pentagons to make half blocks.
Join these together, matching centre seams. Make
both D and L blocks of this kind.

Assembly
Assemble in horizontal strips : L blocks and rectangular D blocks in one strip, D blocks and rectangular L blocks in the other. Join strips with a shift

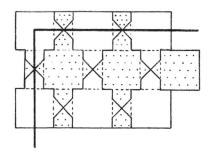

186 Assemble with shift; trim edges

so that pieced blocks come in the middle of plain
blocks above and below them. Trim edges to that one
set of motifs finishes at the edges.

Comments
The jagged diamond pattern is effective and easy,
with little matching, and that at the block stage.

The use of scraps is possible for one of the tones, but
unless each motif is made of the same material, un-
wanted block boundaries will show.

A further pattern can be made by rearranging the
blocks : use two 2 x 4 blocks together, turning the
pairs in alternate rows. Blocks are set straight without
a shift.

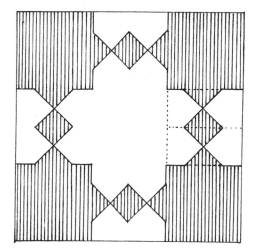

187 Pattern using two 2 x 4 blocks together

ONCE ONLY DESIGNS

Once is definitely enough for some designs. Complicated blocks, or those with a large number of pieces, could form part of a sampler patchwork or could be used individually. They could also form the centre of a medallion or framed patchwork, surrounded by borders of increasing size.

This chapter gives some examples of such designs, with brief notes on assembly.

188   Four linked rings

Linked rings
Both of the linked ring designs need a large number of pieces. Do not plan to make any of the rings the

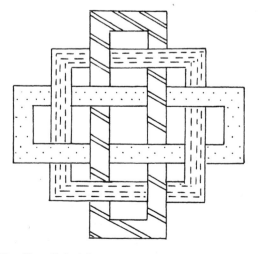

189   Three linked rings

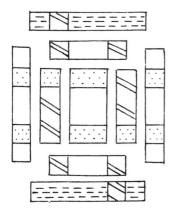

190 Start from the centre (beginning of three rings)

same colour, otherwise the interlace effect will be lost. Start in the centre, and work out, adding pairs of strips to opposite sides in turn. Matching is very important so that there is no discontinuity in the lines of the rings.

The rings can be set straight or on the diagonal; whichever you intend, all piecing must be done straight — for diagonally-placed rings, complete the piecing and then turn the whole round.

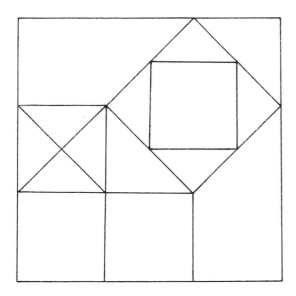

191 Pythagoras

Pythagoras

This is literally geometric patchwork, being a proof of Pythagoras's theorem about the squares on the sides of a right-angled triangle. It is easily assembled from 17 pieces; corners and points must be exactly matched.

Triangles

Another pattern using triangles is based on a diagonally halved square, a simple block but never an easy one to put together with precision. Nine blocks are joined and reflected. I have made this with a black background; the central square is red, and successive triangles working outwards are orange, yellow, green and blue.

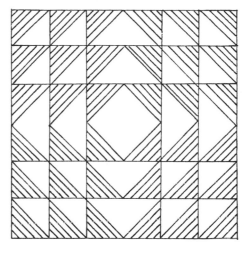

192 Triangles

Op art

Vibrating op art arrangements with strong tonal contrasts rank as once only designs for me because

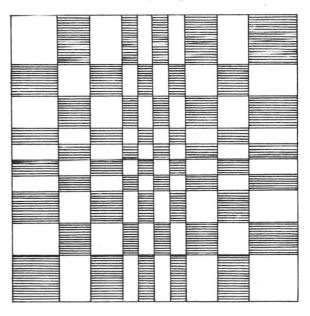

193 Op art design

of the difficulties inherent in the very exact matching necessary. They need a number of templates, all square or rectangular, and are assembled by whichever method you find easiest for matching.

Medallion designs
The remaining designs are all suitable for use as medallion centrepieces.

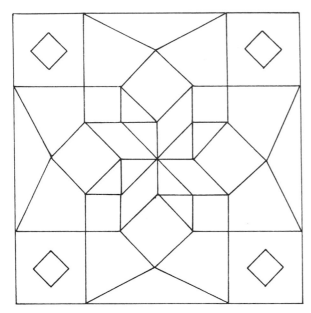

194   Inlaid pattern 1

Inlaid motifs
These are blocks from inlaid patterns observed in Cairo and Alexandria, where they are realised variously in tones of cream, slate, rust and dark brown or black, with the occasional use of turquoise.

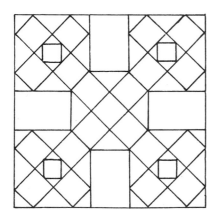

195   Inlaid pattern 2

They can be assembled quite easily, apart from the one with the central octagon. Here, if you want to make a colour contrast between the octagon and the

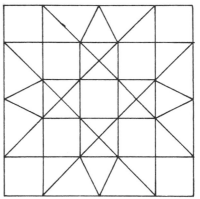

196   Inlaid pattern 3

star points, it is preferable if the eight-pointed star is sewn solid and the central octagon applied by hand, avoiding too many interior joins.

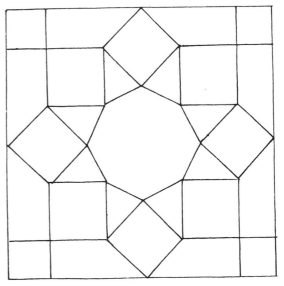

197   Inlaid pattern 4

Developments of basic blocks
Symmetrical developments of basic blocks (with the possible addition of plain blocks or other blocks) can be used on their own and also make good centre-pieces. Anyone can work these out from basic blocks — it is no more than a form of organised doodling.

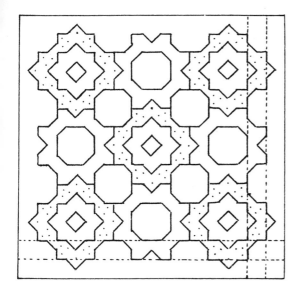

198 From Block 29

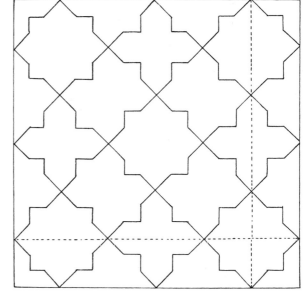

200 From Block 32

199 From Block 30

201 From Block 37

MAKING YOUR OWN BLOCK DESIGNS

When you look around, you find there are patterns everywhere, at least some of them suitable for development into patchwork patterns. If you see a pattern you like, then your task is to find the repeat. Another possibility is to start from a motif and develop it into a pattern. In both cases you must consider whether it is possible to sew the block you want to use.

STARTING FROM AN OBSERVED PATTERN

Note the pattern
The first step is making a note of the lines of the pattern. All but the simplest patterns are difficult to recall without visual support, so even a rough jotting on scrap paper is useful.

Draw it on squared paper
Angles of 45° and right angles need squared paper; 60° angles may fit better on an isometric grid. Draw the pattern out on the appropriate grid.

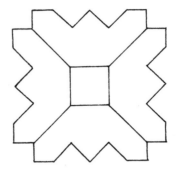

202 a Use squared paper for right angles

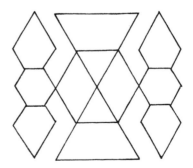

b Use isometric paper for 60° angles

Identify the repeat
There may be an obviously repeated figure in the pattern — colour repeats can help here. Look at the general placement of such figures. If they form

straight vertical and horizontal lines, it is a straight repeat; if they form diagonal lines, you are probably dealing with a dropped or shifted repeat or an alternating arrangement.

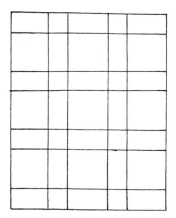

203 a   Straight repeat

b   Vertical rows dropped

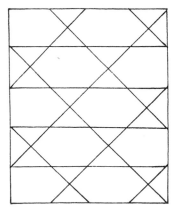

c   Alternate plain blocks

Draw a block

Once you have found the repeat, you are very close to having a block. Rule off a block (square, rectangular or diamond-shaped) to enclose one repeat. Now rule this size of grid all over. The lines should fall in the same relation to subsequent repeats as to the first repeat. Keep on trying till you can see that the blocks are occurring in orderly repetition.

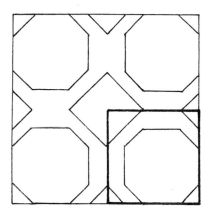

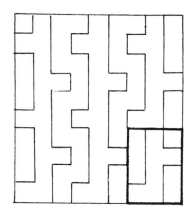

204   Square and rectangular blocks

CAN THE BLOCK BE SEWN ?

You now have a possible block. Whether it is derived (as above) from an observed pattern or is a version of a single motif, the next step is to work out how it can be sewn.

Draw out the lines of the block, and imagine that you are piecing it. Look for lines that cut straight across the block — perhaps it can be assembled from halves or quarters. Symmetrical blocks can often be pieced in reflected quarters (diagram 205).

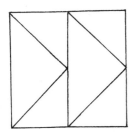

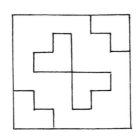

205 a   Assemble in halves
   b   Assemble in quarters

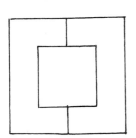

206   Cut the solid area in one

Try to arrange the block so that it has the smallest possible number of pieces, planning to cut solid areas as single units. If necessary, shift the block bound-aries around on the pattern — once the size is right it can be placed anywhere.

Extra joins will have to be added to cope with set-in pieces; also remember the possible use of half open seams.

PATTERNS AND BLOCKS TO AVOID

Avoid patterns with curves, unless they can be modified to give the curved effect with straight lines. Patterns and blocks where lines meet or cross at narrow angles should also be regarded with caution. Try to avoid three-way joins unless they can be pieced without narrow angles.

Some patterns may simply defeat you : the repeat fails to declare itself, or extends over too great an area to be encompassable. Look for patterns you can describe (however imprecisely) in words — this means that the eye has managed to read the pattern.

SOURCES OF MOTIFS

Individual motifs can be found anywhere, including in the very patterns you have given up in despair. Work the motif into a usable block, and develop it into a pattern you like.

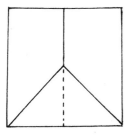

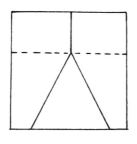

207 a   Extra seam in
      set-in piece

   b   Avoid narrow angles
      (compare *a*)

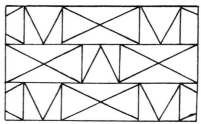

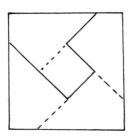

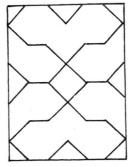

   c   Block using half open seam

208   Letters M (or V, W) and S as lines

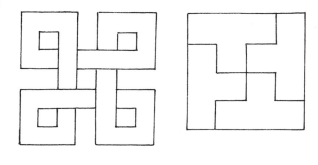

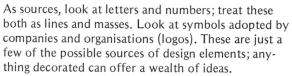

As sources, look at letters and numbers; treat these both as lines and masses. Look at symbols adopted by companies and organisations (logos). These are just a few of the possible sources of design elements; anything decorated can offer a wealth of ideas.

EXEMPLIFICATION

To clarify the whole process of working out how to sew an observed motif let us look at an example and follow it through.

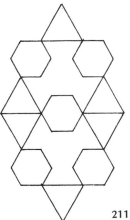

211   Motif from Cairo

209   Letters P, T and E as masses

The motif is from a panel in Manial Palace, Cairo. The angles suggest isometric paper. Part of the motif forms a diamond block, which is drawn out into a pattern.

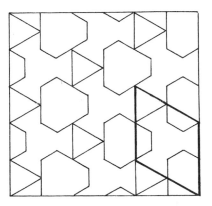

212   Pattern from part-motif

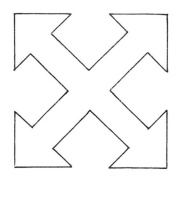

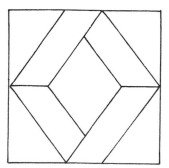

210   Design from logos

A larger diamond block from the whole motif gives a pattern which is an overall repeat of the original.

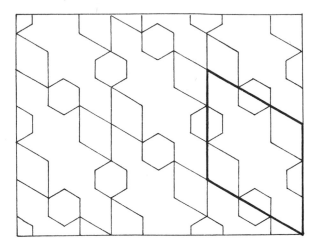

213 Pattern from whole motif

Related squared and isometric designs can be a
fruitful source for the pattern-maker. A squared
version of the part-motif, embellished and reflected,
yields a tile-like pattern. The whole motif squared,
again with added lines, gives a pattern of super-
imposed lattices when reflected.

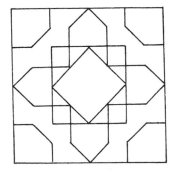

214 Squared version reflected (part-motif)

It is interesting that related patterns from one motif
can appear so different. Note also some shapes and
configurations familiar from other patterns. Such
features of pattern-making help to account for its
endless charm and for the fascination it has exercised
on designers throughout history.

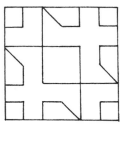

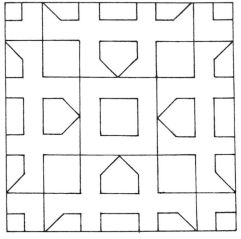

215 Whole motif squared and reflected

PUZZLE PATTERNS

This chapter concludes with a few puzzles — patterns
in which you can try to find the basic repeat, and
consider how best to sew it. Have a fair try at each
pattern before turning to the comments which follow.

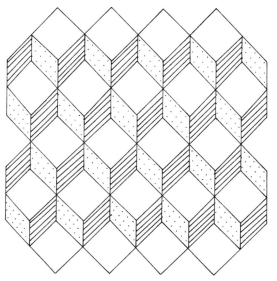

216 Pattern 1

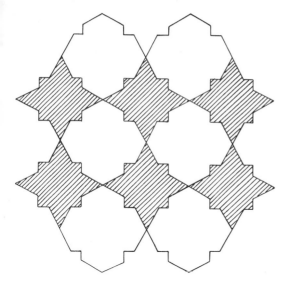

217   Pattern 2

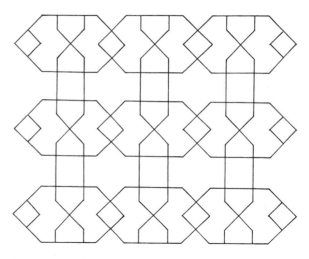

219   Pattern 4

220   Pattern 5

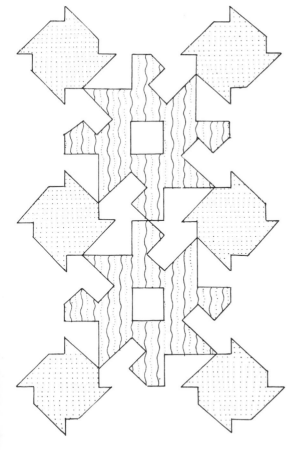

218   Pattern 3

Pattern 1

This is a version of the pattern known as *Boxes* or *Baby's Blocks*.

Piece 2 x 2 blocks with a central diamond with matched pairs of triangles in opposite corners. Assemble with a half shift, matching corners carefully. Use this method to avoid having a seam in the central diamond.

You can also piece strips one unit wide consisting of triangles and alternate dark and light diamonds. This method avoids joins in the long diamonds.

A half-shifted X-block also gives the same pattern, but needs six pieces, and means that all shapes are pieced.

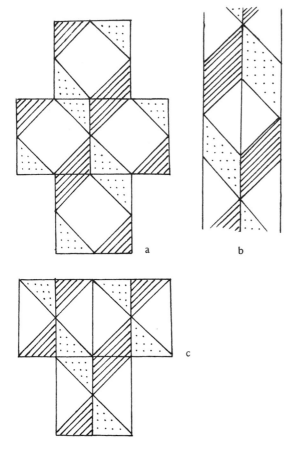

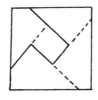

221 Pattern 1 : a 2 x 2 blocks with half shift
 b Strips
 c X-blocks

Pattern 2

A 4 x 4 block produces this easy and effective pattern. You need whole blocks of light and dark, and an easy block with four pieces. Assemble in alternate rows of dark plus horizontal pieced block and vertical pieced block plus light. Compare Block 40.

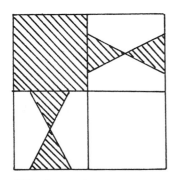

222 Pattern 2 : assembly

Pattern 3

The spiky 10 x 10 flower which is repeated looks unfriendly to piece. Consider it as four blocks (see Block 18) dropped and shifted round a central square, then filled out with rectangles. Using a half open seam, piece the four 4 x 4 blocks and join a rectangle to each. Attach round the square, again starting with a half open seam. Blocks are assembled with a straight repeat.

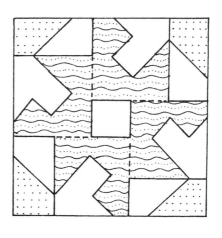

223 Pattern 3 a 10 x 10 block
 b 4 x 4 block and rectangle

Pattern 4

The basic block will be 6 x 6, but how is it best placed? If you think of it as a reflected 3 x 3 block, you will have to use 28 pieces in all (seven in each quarter). This also places seam-joins in the middle of serveral motifs (See diagram 224a.)

Place the boundaries of the block so that they rest as far as possible where there will anyway have to be a seam because of the colours and lines of the pattern. The block shown is made up of four parts : 4 x 4, 4 x 2, 2 x 4 and 2 x 2. Of these, the 4 x 4 part needs

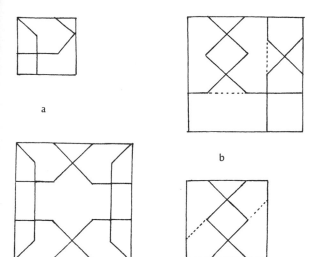

224 Pattern 4 : a 3 x 3 block reflected (28 pieces)
 b Better placing of block (13 pieces)

care : add two seams and assemble in diagonal strips
or using a half open seam. Assemble with straight
repeat. This version of the block has a total of 13
pieces. (See diagram 224 b.)

Pattern 5
Ignore the apparent diagonally-set block. Consider
instead half of the double-ended arrow motif. This
gives a 4 x 4 block which can be easily pieced by
adding joins. Blocks are assembled with alternate
blocks turned 180° (or upside down, if you prefer to
think of it that way). Note that the 4 x 4 block
requires you to use a half-unit measurement; use an
8 x 8 block if you find it easier.

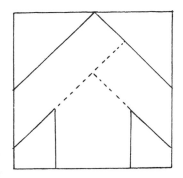

225 Pattern 5 4 x 4 block

FINISHING

Finishing your patchwork will depend on what it is and how it will be used. But whatever the intended use, it will have to be backed to enclose the many raw edges on the back.

BACKING

The easiest and quickest thing to do is simply to back it with material of matching weight to the materials used in the blocks. The colour can either match or contrast.

You may need to piece the backing for large projects, unless you can use a sheet or sheeting, which comes in generous widths. If you are using new material, wash and iron it before use.

Having assembled the patchwork, with or without borders as wanted, press it and lay it evenly face up on a flat surface. This may well be a clean floor. Piece or cut the backing so that it is the same size, ie finished size plus seam allowances. Lay the backing on the patchwork, right side down, and smooth it so that all edges correspond. Pin amply, starting in the middle and working out to the edges, which should be pinned all round a short distance from the seam line. You may prefer to tack after pinning so that the pins can be removed before sewing.

Before you start sewing, check that the bobbin thread is not about to run out — wind a new one if necessary. Stitch round three and a half sides on the seam line,

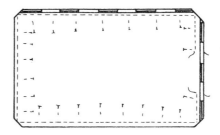

226   Stitch round leaving an opening for turning

starting before a corner and finishing after one, so that about half a side, or less, remains open. Trim diagonally across corners, and turn the whole thing right side out. The corners may have to be pushed out from inside to make them square — use a crochet hook or a knitting needle and avoid anything sharp, like scissor points, that might make a hole. The open edges can now be joined : press in the seam allowance, pin or tack and slip-stitch closed by hand. You can run a line of top-stitching round all the sides to give a firm edge.

This is a minimum adequate way of finishing. Sometimes known as 'bag' assembly, it can be used for bed-covers, cushion or pillow covers and other household items like tablecloths. If you want some extra weight in a bed covering, back with prequilted material. All bed coverings hang better at the foot of the bed if the two bottom corners are rounded off; this conflicts with borders, so plan accordingly.

QUILTING

If you want to quilt, then your work is not nearly done when the patchwork itself is complete. Quilting is a craft in its own right, and this part of your work should not be regarded as subordinate. Close quilting may take longer than the piecing and assembly of the blocks. Unlike patchwork, quilting can really only be done satisfactorily by hand.

Supplies for quilting
You need wadding or batting for quilting; old blankets can be used too, but there should be no uneven wear. Man-made wadding of terylene, dacron or polyester fibres is available in various weights/thicknesses. The thicker the wadding, the more the quilting will show. In the UK wadding is bought by the metre, and comes in 1 m (39 in) widths; in the US batting comes in sizes suitable for large and small quilts.

Assembling for quilting
You will probably have to use more than one width if you have bought wadding by the metre. Place the edges together, and join with large, loose, diagonal stitches — an overlapped seam with tight stitches would make a hard ridge which would show up. The size should be that of the patchwork.

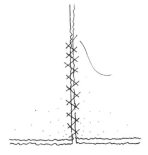

227   Joining wadding

To assemble, piece or cut backing fabric so that it is a little larger all round than the patchwork. This backing material should not be lighter in weight than the front of the quilt, or else there is a danger that the quilting will be more prominent on the back than the front. Place backing on a large flat surface like a

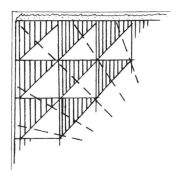

228   Tacking for quilting

clean floor, face down. The wadding or batting goes on top, centred, and finally the patchwork, face up and likewise centred. Smooth so that everything is lying flat. Pin carefully from the centre outwards, being sure to catch all three layers. Tack or baste all over — this is a necessity and not an option for quilting. Remove pins, and you are ready to start the actual quilting.

Quilting
For large projects a quilting frame is indispensable. A frame holds the quilt in even tension and the layers

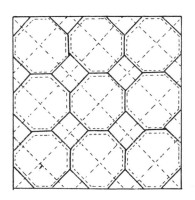

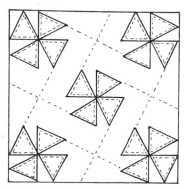

229   Outline quilting with added lines relating to the patch-work pattern

cannot move around. Smaller projects can be quilted without a frame.

For quilting patterns, see some of the books mentioned in the bibliography. I often quilt close to seams to throw part of the pattern into relief — this is called outline quilting. For this I generally try to match the colour of the thread to that of the motif being outlined. A single neutral colour of thread can be used for allover quilting; it must be strong, because you do not want your quilting stitches to break and come undone. Use thin crochet cotton or a comparable weight. Quilting stitches are simple running stitches, done as evenly and regularly as you can. They should be short, as longer stitches can catch and pull. A thimble is indispensable, so try to master its use for quilting, even if you never otherwise use one.

This extremely brief account of quilting is meant as no more than an idication of what is involved. Detailed accounts can be found elsewhere, generally in publications originating in the US, where patchwork and quilting are still closely associated. In Britain the two seem to have diverged.

Finishing after quilting
When you have completed the work of quilting, it still remains for you to finish the piece. The edges are still raw. You have a choice of ways of finishing. You can turn the top ie the patchwork over the edges to the back, turn it in, and hand stitch down all round. In the case of a pieced top where the blocks extend to the edges without a border, you will lose some of the pattern. With borders you will avoid this, but the width of the border should take this possibility into account, or else the quilt will be smaller than planned. You can do the opposite — bring the backing to the front, forming an extra narrow border, turn it in and stitch it down. You can turn both edges in so that they meet in the middle, and stitch them together. Or you can add a binding of bias tape or strips of material, contrasting or matching. This can be machined to the backing and caught in place by hand stitching on the front, or vice versa.

TYING

You may want to make something with the added warmth of a layer of stuffing, but without the extra work of quilting. The answer is tying, which serves to hold the stuffing in place, the original function of quilting stitches.

To tie, take two or three stitches in the same place with strong thread, working straight up and down

230   Reef knot or flat knot

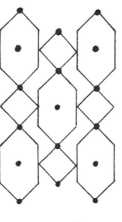

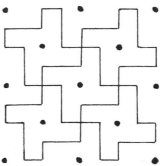

231   Tying patterns

through all layers; knot the ends of the thread at front or back in a reef knot (flat or square knot). To make this, pass the right thread over the left and then under, then the left thread over the right and under. Knots should be regularly spaced not more than about 15 cm (6 in) apart, and should stand in some relation to the patchwork pattern, eg. at block joins or motif centres or intersections.

BACKING AND MOUNTING HANGINGS

Patchwork makes interesting wall-hangings. These can be soft-mounted, ie without any stiffening, or hard-mounted on a rigid surface.

Soft hangings
For soft wall hangings, sew backing and patchwork with right sides facing as for bag assembly above. Do not forget to leave a space for turning. Add or stitch a channel or tabs to hold a rod at the top. The rod can

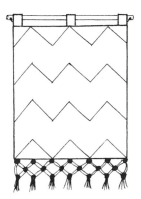

232　Tabs for hanging; an added fringe

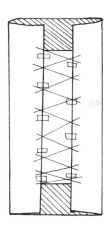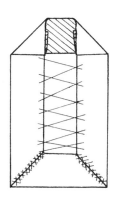

233　Two stages in mounting work on a board

be balanced on two wall nails or tacks, one at each
end, or you can attach a string so that it hangs from a
single nail. Some pieces hang better with a weight at
the bottom; another rod can be slipped through tabs
sewn onto the back for this purpose. Trim or decor-
ate as desired — a row of tassels may add a suitable
finishing touch, or you might like to add a macramé
fringe. A hanging you want to quilt is quilted first
and then finished like a quilt.

Rigid mounting
There are several ways in which a piece of patchwork
may be rigidly mounted. A professional picture-
framer will handle the whole job for you. The framer
will be able to advise if extra borders should be sewn
round the edge of the piece to avoid obscuring any of
the pattern in mounting. Choose non-reflecting glass
if you must have the piece glazed, but patchwork,
like all sewing, is more effective unglazed.

You can mount patchwork yourself on a piece of
hardboard (masonite) or timber. The thinner the rigid
mount, the easier it will be to get the corners to lie
prettily. You will need to sew extra margins of at
least 5 - 8 cm (2 - 3 in) to all sides of the piece, unless
you do not mind losing some areas of pattern at the
edges. Cut the board to size. Mark lightly on the back
of the patchwork the areas you want to show. Press.
You may want to pad the front of the board lightly
with a sheet of foam rubber or some fabric (old
blankets are useful for this). Anchor foam or fabric
with a dab of glue.

Lay the patchwork face down on a flat surface;
centre the board over it, matching edges to the marks
on the patchwork. Turn over a long side of the patchwork, and hold it in place with tape; do the same to
the opposite side, keeping it taut. Now sew these two
sides into place, taking long stitches between them,
and using doubled or very strong thread.

When this has been done you can turn over the top
and bottom edges, folding them in as you do when
making a parcel. It will take a bit of worrying at them
to get them to lie tidily. Pin or tape them into place,
and then stitch as before.

Rings for hanging can be stitched on, about a quarter
or a third of the way from both sides, and a hanging
cord attached between them. Heavier pieces will need
screw eyes, which go into an extra strip of wood
attached to the board before mounting the patchwork. You can neaten the back by gluing on a piece
of cardboard, cut to size (use adhesive hanging hooks
in this case).

Sheets of polystyrene can also be used succesfully for
mounting. Make a 'bag' of patchwork and backing,
leaving it open the entire length of one side. Slip in
the polystyrene carefully, and close the open side
by hand stitching.

Junk polystyrene used for packaging can be used
to mount work. Long pins inserted at an angle hold
the piece in place. One disadvantage is that the
polystyrene shapes are often fat from back to front,
which makes difficulties with the corners.

A final and more traditional way of mounting is to
use a square or rectangular wooden frame over which
the patchwork is stretched, and to which it is tacked
from behind. Tape, braid or dowelling give a framed
effect.

USES AND APPLICATIONS OF PATCHWORK

Traditionally, patchwork has often been used to make bed coverings. However there is no need to restrict its use to this single household item. As well as making bed covers of all sizes and for all ages (a pram cover is a rewarding size to start on), you can find a use for patchwork in every room in the house.

Chairs and stools can have patchwork covers, removable for washing; tablecloths and mats can be made, to say nothing of tea-cosies, long-time favourites of hand-patchworkers. Cushion and pillow covers are easy and quick; I have made a cover for a foam-rubber bathmat : it looks nice and slips on and off easily for washing. Children like patchwork, specially if it contains material from outgrown clothes — you could make patchwork curtains for small windows (also for big ones, but the scale of work is intimidating).

Many small items can be quickly and cheaply made in patchwork. You can make bags of all descriptions : shopping bags, shoe bags, laundry bags, toy bags, beach bags, evening bags. A length of patchwork makes a good cover for a sewing machine or a typewriter when you have to stop working, but do not want to put the machine away. You could even make a shaped cover for a sewing machine. Extra blocks, or blocks which had to be discarded, can be made into pot-holders for the kitchen — no one grabbing a hot handle will ever notice that the triangle points do not quite meet.

Perhaps the only problem is where to stop. For most of us it is probably wise to draw the line at clothes made entirely of patchwork. Even unquilted, patchwork when backed is bulky, and it is difficult to find garments which are still attractive when made up in patchwork.

One piece of clothing which is successful in patchwork is a waistcoat (vest) — this can even be quilted. Otherwise, patchwork can be used for trimming and decoration : round the hem of a long skirt, in yokes or pockets of dresses or shirts (line to cover the raw edges). Aprons, coveralls and bibs can also be trimmed with patchwork, or even made entirely from it.

It is also easy to apply pieced patchwork for decorative purposes, using normal appliqué methods. Pieced motifs or blocks are stitched directly to a ground material, and therefore little extra bulk is added.

For hand attachment (by buttonhole or hem stitch), the outer edges of the piece for application are turned in by the amount of the seam allowance (trim if this is wide) and pressed. Pin or tack the patchwork into place, and sew down.

For machine application, trim off most of the seam allowance, tack into position, and go round the outline with straight stitch. Cover this with satin stitch, and trim off any projecting material with small scissors.

Just as the choice of patterns from blocks is very wide, so is the choice of what you do with your patchwork. You have been given some starting points, and now you are on your own, pursuing the tradition of individuality which has always been such an important feature in the history of patchwork.

BIBLIOGRAPHY

RECOMMENDED BOOKS

USA

GUTCHEON, BETH, *The Perfect Patchwork Primer*, Penguin Books, 1974, first published by McKay, New York, 1973
This detailed account of every stage of machine pie-cing, generally of traditional blocks, is very good on the making of templates and the process of quilting. It includes instructions for using patchwork in fashion and other items. Probably the most useful all-round book in the list, it is interestingly different in style and approach from other books on the subject.

ICKIS, MARGUERITE, *The Standard Book of Quilt Making and Collecting*, Dover Publications, New York, 1959 (published in UK by Constable)
This unaltered re-publication of an original 1949 work includes a full account of all aspects of quilt making (containing extensive information — with patterns — on quilting) with over 200 patterns. A short section on colour choice is given mostly in terms of surroundings. Some templates are given, also instructions for the traditional folded paper method of drafting patterns. It concludes with a brief history of quilt making.

LARSEN, JUDITH, and GULL, CAROL, *The Patch-work Quilt Design and Coloring Book*, Butterick, New York, 1977
Gives exact instructions for making quilts, with total yardage needed and full size templates, for a number of traditional patterns. Useful section on colour and design, with blank grids provided for trying out colourings.

MCKIM, RUBY, *One Hundred and One Patchwork Patterns*, Dover Publications, New York, 1962 (published in UK by Constable)
This is a revised version of a work originally published in 1931. It offers a range of appliqué and pieced blocks, many suitable for machine piecing. All tem-plates are given and can be traced off. Useful sections on Materials, Cutting and Piecing, Setting, Borders and Quilting (with patterns) are scattered among the blocks and may be difficult to locate (no index is given except of block names).

UK

COLBY, AVERIL, *Patchwork*, Batsford, 1958, paperback 1976

Claimed to be the definitive work on the technique, design and history of patchwork, this book gives a detailed account, with many photographs, of the development of hand patchwork in Britain. Includes information on techniques using different shapes, also appliqué and the making of templates. Fine background reading for anyone interested in patchwork.

FARNSWORTH, RUTH (ed), *Patchwork and Appliqué*, Marshall Cavendish, 1972
Gives detailed instructions, with many coloured photographs, in the techniques of patchwork, both pieced and applied, using patterns from both Britain and America. Yardages are given for a number of specific projects.

PYMAN, KIT (ed), *Patchwork*, Search Press, 1978
Very short (32pp) introduction to patchwork, usefully illustrated with coloured photographs and diagrams. Not really concerned with machine patchwork, but includes a not dismissive mention. Worth its modest price. See also *Quilting* in the same (*Needle Crafts*) series, although this does not deal specifically with the quilting of patchwork.

RICHARDSON, ROSAMOND, and GRIFFITHS, ERICA, *Discovering Patchwork*, BBC, 1977
Accompanied a TV series of the same name (1978). A well-balanced account, profusely illustrated, of techniques for hand and machine patchwork. Includes a section on template-making, and detailed instructions for making a variety of items using over 70 traditional British and American patterns. Written for the beginner, it nevertheless offers in compact form much to interest anyone making patchwork.

OTHER BOOKS ON PATCHWORK

Among the large number of books available on patchwork, these might also be consulted :

BISHOP, R., and SAFANDA, E., *A Gallery of Amish Quilts*, Phaidon Press and Dutton, 1976

IVES, SUZY, *Ideas for Patchwork*, Batsford, 1974

SCHOENFELD, SUSAN, *Pattern Design for Needlepoint and Patchwork*, Van Nostrand, 1974

TIMMINS, ALICE, *Introducing Patchwork*, Batsford, 1972

BOOKS ON DESIGN

CHRISTIE, ARCHIBALD H., *Pattern Design, an Introduction to the Study of Formal Arrangement*, Dover Publications, New York, 1969 (published in UK by Constable)

EL-SAID, ISSAM, and PARMAN, AYŞE, *Geometric Concepts in Islamic Art*, World of Islam Festival Publishing Company, London, 1976

HILL, DEREK (photographs), and GRABAR, OLEG (introductory text), *Islamic Architecture and its Decoration*, Faber and Faber, second edition 1967

Ensor Holliday's *Altair Designs* (Longman, 1972) are also of interest. These are computer-aided grids based on traditional design principles, intended for colouring in.

LIST OF SUPPLIERS

UK

Material for patchwork

Laura Ashley shops in many towns and cities offer a choice of small-scale prints and solids in good colours, by the metre and in packets of patchwork pieces. Information from :

Laura Ashley
30 Great Oak Street, Llanidloes, Powys, Wales

Remnant parcels of printed cottons and polyester cottons are available from :

J W Coates and Co Ltd
Albert Street Warehouse, Nelson, Lancs BB9 7EZ

Wadding and pre-quilted material

Department stores eg John Lewis Partnership, and fabric shops.

Squared and isometric paper

Good stationers, and shops supplying architects and draughtsmen (ask for Chartwell products). Dressmaking paper from sewing and needlework departments of stores. By mail order (not isometric paper) from :

ESA Creative Learning
Pinnacles, P O Box 22, Harlow, Essex CM19 5AY

and (including isometric paper) :

E J Arnold and Son Ltd
Butterley Street, Leeds LS10 1AX

US

Patchwork supplies

Mountain Mist quilt patterns, cotton and polyester batting, blueprint for quilting frame and other patchwork and quilting supplies (catalogue $1.50) by mail order from :

The Stearns and Foster Company
P O Box 15380, Lockland, Cincinatti, Ohio 45215

Precut patchwork pieces, quilted material, quilting frames and different weights and sizes of batting available from stores and by mail order from catalogue:

Sears Roebuck and Co
4640 Roosevelt Boulevard, Philadelphia Pa. 19132

INDEX

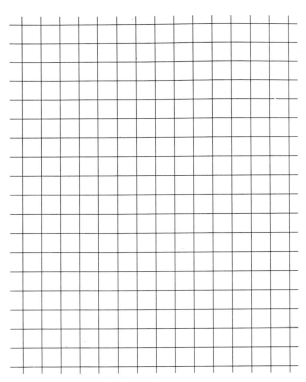

A   5 mm squares

B   5 cm squares with diagonals

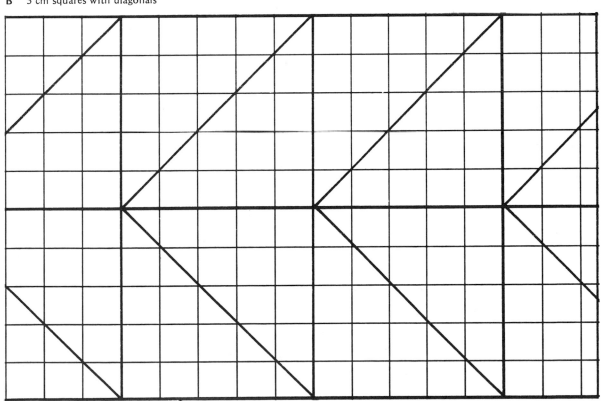

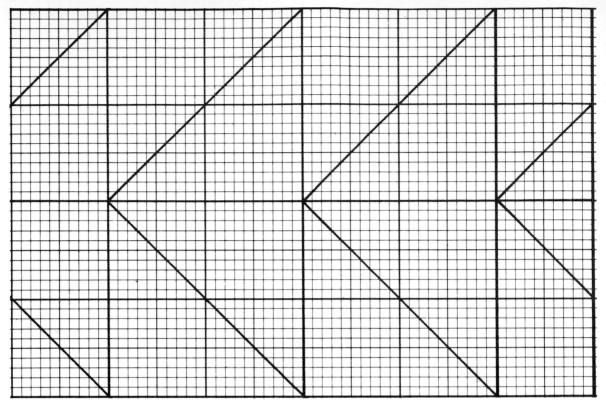

C   2 in squares with diagonals

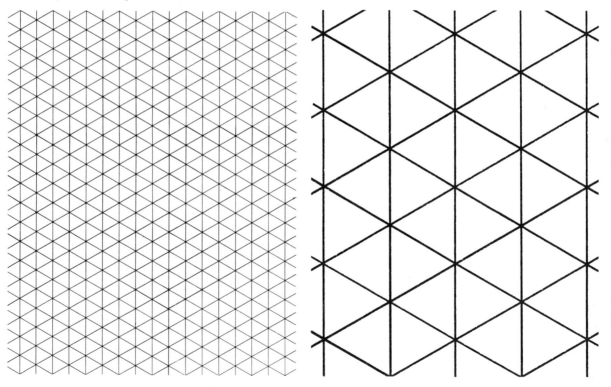

D   5 mm isometric grid

E   2 cm isometric grid